A NATION
of SHEEP

Dedicated to the memory
of
THOMAS HARDING JONES,
born on June 12th 1950,
died on July 31st 2007.
May the angels carry you,
my dear friend,
into Paradise.

ALSO BY ANDREW P. NAPOLITANO

Constitutional Chaos:
What Happens When Government Breaks Its Own Laws

The Constitution in Exile:
How the Federal Government Has Seized Power by
Rewriting the Supreme Law of the Land

CONTENTS

CONTENTS

INTRODUCTION

P icture this: The Attorney General of the United States testifies under oath that the president is not ordering federal agents to read the mail, listen to the telephone calls, and monitor the computer keystrokes of ordinary Americans, without a warrant to do so from a judge. That would be criminal. But six months later, the president admits that he has done so.

Picture this: The Constitution prohibits Congress from abridging free speech. But suddenly, Congress has made it a crime to talk about receiving self-written search warrants from an FBI agent.

Picture this: The Constitution guarantees speedy, fair jury trials with defense counsel, but all of the sudden, Congress authorizes the president to dispense with those rights if the U.S. military has incarcerated you in Cuba.

And one more: The Constitution guarantees that the government can only force you to sell your house to it if it plans a public use of the property. But now the Supreme Court is telling the government it can sell your house to your neighbor, against your will.

These are not Hollywood movie plots but recent, unhappy history. They are just a few events in the sad history of liberty lost to an out-of-control government that we have sheepishly permitted to subvert our rights.

But, are not our rights *guaranteed* by the Constitution? Why doesn't anyone in government take seriously the oath to uphold the Constitution? Why does it seem that every time you listen to the president, he is asking for more power and authority from Congress to invade our privacy, stifle our speech, and shortcut prosecutions? Is there any limit on the powers that Congress can give the president, or that the president can just seize and exercise? Can the Supreme Court simply change well-regarded rules so as to allow the government to seize your house and sell it to your neighbor? Do we have any rights, as human beings or as Americans, that the government cannot take away, no matter what its goal may be?

These questions do not have simple or direct answers. But they are questions that all who love liberty should be asking. I have written this book to generate a debate about freedom; a debate, regrettably, that government does not want us to have. Now, why do I say that? Well, President Bush has argued that his job is to "protect the homeland" because "our government's greatest responsibility is to protect the American people. That's our most important job,"[1] and thus, all that he does toward that goal, in his view, is good and appropriate. Even when he silences opponents, strips innocents of their dignity, disregards federal criminal law, establishes military courts, unseen by Americans since the Civil War, and rejects the freedoms *guaranteed* in the Constitution, he claims he is doing his job. And his Administration has argued that there should be no debate about any of this, because debate itself helps "the enemy" and thus impairs the government's ability to protect the homeland.

But is protecting "the homeland"—Teutonic as that sounds— just a matter of protecting human beings from physical harm? Or is there more to it than that? Should not the government also be responsible for protecting our values and the freedoms we are guaranteed in the United States Constitution? If you read the oath that every president has taken, as it is prescribed in the Constitution, you will quickly see what the Founding Fathers established as the president's principal job: to uphold, preserve, protect, and defend *the Constitution*. Yet today, in an attempt to protect our lives, the

> **Here's another profound question: How can government possibly preserve freedom by taking it away? Answer: The government is not interested in preserving freedom, and it has stated as much.**

Constitution is being violated—on a daily basis, it seems—as more and more of our freedoms are taken away. Among well-meaning persons, the government's primary responsibility is in dispute.

This dispute—is the government's primary job to protect our lives or our freedoms?—is more than academic. The answer to the question determines whether our freedoms are ours to keep, or the government's for the taking.

Here's another profound question: How can government possibly preserve freedom by taking it away? Answer: The government is not interested in preserving freedom, and it has stated as much. The president must presume that protection of our real estate ranks higher than protection of the Constitution, even though his oath is to uphold the latter. Notwithstanding the current president's oath, "registered in Heaven," as one of his notorious predecessors liked to say, the Bush Administration has systematically attacked and diminished virtually every freedom and right guaranteed by the Constitution: freedom of speech, freedom of the press, freedom of religion, freedom of association, the right to privacy, the right not to self-incriminate, the right to counsel, the right to speedy trials, the right to fair trials, the right to avoid cruel and unusual punishment, even the right to be set free after *acquittal*! All of these liberties have suffered egregiously since September 11th 2001. President Bush has broken laws he swore to uphold, and declined to enforce laws that he has himself signed into existence, all in the name of making us safer.

> It is only when we become as sheep, out of fear, complacency, or weakness, that we lose the love of freedom. And when the love of freedom dies, there can be no hope for joy. No one can be happy and unfree.

The president and Congress, with Republicans, Democrats, liberals, and conservatives concurring, have persuaded the American people that by voluntarily giving up the freedoms we love and cherish, the government will keep us safe.

If we look to the Founding Fathers, we can see how they rejected that idea. They believed that "those who would give up essential Liberty to purchase a little temporary Safety, deserve neither Liberty nor Safety."[2] They announced, "Give me liberty or give me death." And they proclaimed, "When the people fear the government, there is tyranny. When the government fears the people, there is liberty." Our forefathers fully understood that the goal of government must be to preserve freedom, and that failure to do so undermines the reason we have created a government. Free individuals, standing firm, demanding that their governments protect natural rights, and insisting on the right to be left alone, can only be denied by tyrants, not by those faithful to the Constitution.

It is only when we become as sheep, out of fear, complacency, or weakness, that we lose the love of freedom. And when the love of freedom dies, there can be no hope for joy. No one can be happy and unfree.

Would you rather be "safe" but unfree? Not me. I'd rather die fighting for freedom than live as a slave. And in this book, I'll show you why.

1

WHERE DOES FREEDOM COME FROM?

In order to understand our constitutional rights and their importance in our lives, we must understand their origins. Although these rights have always been the subject of controversy, our country's founding documents—the Constitution and the Declaration of Independence—show that the men we call our founders generally agreed that the fundamental freedoms traditionally attributable to those who live in a democracy are God-given rights inherent in our humanity. Sadly, in the administrations of virtually every American president, from George Washington to George W. Bush, the government that was formed to protect these basic rights has rejected the significance of our humanity in enforcing the laws, in legislating, and in conducting trials. At all levels of the government, legislators and judges and lawyers and law enforcement officials have become infected with a fad in legal theory that favors the laws created to benefit the few, regardless of the impact on the fundamental rights common to everyone.

IT'S ONLY NATURAL . . .

Scholars usually divide legal theories of the origin of our rights into two fundamental camps. Individuals in the first camp believe that the law goes beyond man-made rules and that we are the beneficiaries of a universal body of laws. Laws that do not respect these universal laws, they argue, are not laws at all. These people subscribe to what is called "natural law."

Natural law teaches that the law extends from human nature, which is created by God. The natural law states that because all humans desire freedom from artificial restraint, and because all human beings yearn to be free, our freedoms stem from our very humanity and, ultimately, from the Creator of humanity.

Natural law is not linked to a particular religion, or to religion at all, necessarily. The ideas simply include rights and rules beyond those written or used by government officials. It recognizes that as human beings, we must have a core set of liberties in order to live just and peaceful lives. Humanity is the basis for these rights, and therefore they are common to all of us.

These liberties belong to us by virtue of our nature, and they persist in spite of any action the government may take against them, regardless of alleged necessity or majority rule. Supreme Court Justice Clarence Thomas has remarked that "natural rights and higher law arguments are the best defense of liberty and of limited government." Moreover, he continues, "without recourse to higher law, we abandon our best defense of judicial review—a judiciary active in defending the Constitution. Rather than being a justification for the worst type of judicial activism, higher law is [the] only alternative to the willfulness of both run-amok majorities [in Congress] and run-amok judges [in federal courts]."[1]

Today we face the constant threat of surrendering too much of our natural freedom out of fear of terrorism and a desire for national security. I often hear well-intentioned and even well-educated Americans saying that we need to balance liberty and security, that hard or threatening times should produce less freedom and thus more security. I've even had some crackpots tell me on the air that they are fearful of freedom and yearn for more security. This argument presumes that the same government that can't deliver the mail, can't fill potholes, can't keep track of who has paid taxes, and can't obey its own laws should somehow be trusted to limit and even proscribe our freedoms, and that giving them this power will keep us safe. This is a canard, a pact with the devil, a one-way trip into slavery that is as old as the idea of having a government.

Liberty and security are not to be balanced; liberty is the default position because it is integral to our nature. Every conceivable bias is to be indulged in its favor; *all* of our liberties are to be protected by security. As Supreme Court Justice Robert Jackson wrote, "Implicit in the term 'national defense' is the notion of defending those values and ideas which set this Nation apart . . . It would indeed be ironic if, in the name of national defense, we would sanction the subversion of . . . those liberties . . . which make the defense of the Nation worthwhile."[2]

Benjamin Franklin once famously said, "Those who would give up essential Liberty, to purchase a little temporary Safety, deserve neither Liberty nor Safety."[3] He obviously meant that those who give up freedom in the hope of security will end up with neither, because a government strong enough to take your freedom away from

> Liberty and security are not to be balanced; liberty is the default position because it is integral to our nature.

you, just because your fearful neighbors want to give up theirs, cannot be expected to return it. The liberties inherent in the natural law are the only justification for laws aimed at security.

Martin Luther King Jr. also adhered to natural law philosophy. In his famous "Letter from Birmingham Jail," King described the connection between natural law and justice: "How does one determine whether a law is just or unjust? A just law is a man-made code that squares with the moral law or the law of God. An unjust law is a code that is out of harmony with the moral law. To put it in the terms of St. Thomas Aquinas: "An unjust law is a human law that is not rooted in eternal law and natural law. Any law that uplifts human personality is just. Any law that degrades human personality is unjust."[4]

Many people reject the claim that we have rights beyond the decrees of government officials. Critics have bellowed that it is difficult to determine what natural law requires in specific situations. Natural liberties might be said to include a number of different particular rights, such as the right to privacy or to free speech, which could in turn be enforced in many ways. The debate over which liberties might count as part of the natural law, and how they ought to be enforced, has baffled thinkers and lawmakers since the theory was introduced. This bafflement has led some to prefer to follow and discuss a *written* law, even an unjust one, so long as it is written down.

This difficulty has led many critics to question the role of natural law in our legal system. Partly due to laziness and partly because of the attractiveness of the academically trendy alternative, known as "positivism," anti–natural law scholars have failed to grasp the obvious truth of the nature of our government: It is founded on the belief that individual liberties are permanent; Jefferson called them "unalienable." An *unalienable* right comes from God and is an element of humanity that cannot be given up or legislated away.

> **An unalienable right comes from God and is an element of humanity that cannot be given up or legislated away.**

The rights of our cousins in Europe were first recognized when the great monarchies began to fall. Think about it: government "giving" liberty. In America, the government first came about because *free individuals gave it power*. This was the opposite of Europe, where monarchial governments "permitted" individuals to enjoy liberty. Law does not create "right" and "wrong" in matters of liberty and freedom; it recognizes them as boundaries, as an aid to guiding us to justice.

Critics of natural law should read the Declaration of Independence. It recognizes more freedom than all of the government-written laws combined.

It's not surprising that Jefferson and his fellow authors of the Declaration of Independence believed in the natural law. Intellectuals and statesmen have adhered to the natural law for thousands of years, dating back to ancient Greeks and Romans such as Aristotle and Cicero. Cicero, the premier Roman lawyer, reflected that "right is based, not upon man's opinion, but upon Nature." And Aristotle, one of the greatest minds of ancient Greece, argued that "one part of what is politically just is natural, and the other part is legal."

In drafting the Declaration of Independence, Thomas Jefferson was influenced by two prominent English thinkers: John Locke and Thomas Paine. He borrowed considerably from the language and philosophies of both men in drafting the Declaration. For example, both Locke and Paine used the word *unalienable* to describe human rights.

Locke, in his *Second Treatise on Government*, wrote, "Reason . . .

teaches all Mankind . . . that being all equal and independent, no one ought to harm another in his Life, Health, Liberty, or Possessions."[5] That immunity from harm includes harm caused by government— language and thoughts clearly echoed in the Declaration and its understanding of natural rights.

In *The Rights of Man*, Paine wrote that these natural rights include "all the intellectual rights, or rights of the mind, and also all those rights of acting as an individual for his own comfort and happiness, which are not injurious to the natural rights of others."[6] The government, argued Jefferson, Locke, and Paine, can only do what is necessary to secure and protect those rights, and it can only use powers granted to it by those who formed it. This is what is meant by "the consent of the governed."[7]

To follow natural law is not to say that all rights are natural; many rights do come from the state. The right to drive a motor vehicle on a government-owned roadway is a state-granted right; hence, the government can lawfully regulate it (by requiring a driver's license, limiting speed, etc.) and lawfully take it away (for example, from habitual drunk drivers).

The fact that freedom comes not from government, not from the consent of the governed, not from the community, but from God and is inherent to our humanity has profound effects on the way all modern governments work. It means that our basic freedoms, such as freedom of the press, freedom of speech, and the right to privacy (which, although not named explicitly in the Constitution, is implied in at least ten places), cannot be disregarded by the government unless we are convicted of violating natural law—in other words, someone else's freedoms—and the government can only convict us if it follows what is called "procedural due process."

Procedural due process means that we know in advance of the

violations of natural law that the government will prosecute, that we are fully notified by the government of the charges against us, that we have a fair trial with counsel before a truly neutral judge and jury, that we can confront and challenge the government's evidence against us, that we can summon persons and evidence on our own behalf, that the government must prove our misdeeds beyond a reasonable doubt, and that we have the right to appeal the outcome of that trial to another neutral judge. As you will shortly see,

> **Our present government has made every attempt to thwart our right to due process, using claims of national security and state secrets to mask the use of truly dictatorial powers and procedures, profoundly contrary to the natural law.**

our present government has made every attempt to thwart our right to due process, using claims of national security and state secrets to mask the use of truly dictatorial powers and procedures, profoundly contrary to the natural law.

POSITIVISM: POSITIVE OR NEGATIVE?

The other camp of legal theorists, the so-called positivists, does not accept the connection between humanity and liberty. These theorists care only for the pedigree of the law and the lawmaker; as long as a law is made according to the rules, by an accepted lawmaker, it is the law. Under positivism, the law is whatever those in power say it is, whether that decision is democratic or dictatorial in nature. Under positivism, whoever or whatever controls the government, whether a majority or a minority, always rules and always gets its way.

Positivism is perhaps the most primitive legal theory, having evolved only slightly from the sort of justification that could be offered for following the demands of a tribal chieftain or general-turned-dictator. The theory promotes fear rather than respect.

In this camp, anyone with the power to intimidate his community, such as Hitler under the Nazi regime, can create a law. Positivists are faced with the tough choice of following all the laws, even those made by genocidal dictators, or figuring out a way to explain why the letter of the law should not be followed in isolated cases, without referring to natural law.

To a positivist, the government's goal is to bring about the greatest benefit to the greatest number of people. Under the natural law, the only legitimate goal of government is to secure liberty, which is the freedom to obey one's own free will and conscience, rather than the free wills or consciences of others.

The problem today in America, the greatest and gravest threat to personal freedom in this country, is that the positivists are carrying the day. Under their sway, the government violates the law while busily passing more legislation to abridge our liberties.

However, the significance of natural law has not escaped even the Bush Administration. Natural law, as we have seen, is the basis for our liberty, inspiring the men who drafted the Declaration of Independence and the Constitution. So President Bush has also publicly supported natural law, but unlike Jefferson before him, his statements amount to lip service. At his 2005 inaugural address, President Bush declared, "From the day of our founding, we have proclaimed that every man and woman on this Earth has rights and dignity and matchless value, because they bear the image of the Maker of heaven and Earth."[8] The chapters in this book will demonstrate that President Bush's professed adherence to natural law principles is merely a pretense, the same pretense adhered to by virtually all of his predecessors. You will soon discover the federal government's sinister history of twisting our "rights and dignity and matchless value" to serve its own ends: To appropriate more and more power for itself.

Unfortunately, the majority of us tolerate these plots for control. We vote carelessly and acquiesce to impeachable offenses, allowing the government to quash our liberties and ignore our rights. And because we're busy panicking about terrorism, we neglect to notice that the positivist legal community is using our fear to its advantage. By virtue of the majority vote, the positivists among us are able to write and pass unconstitutional laws, give dangerous powers to public officials, and sap our liberties, all without most people recognizing what has been done to them.

To undo the damage done by all three branches of the federal government, we must vote for and encourage representatives who respect the natural law. We must also engage in open political debate to find ways to promote our natural freedoms. We must not surrender our rights like sheep if we are to uphold the American spirit of rugged individualism.

It is my hope and purpose in writing this book that the good folks who read it will recognize that the government is not our friend, that the gravest dangers to our freedoms lie hidden in a government that has seized them from us, and that vigilance and adherence to natural law can save us from the power-hungry bureaucrats who run the government today.

> We must not surrender our rights like sheep if we are to uphold the American spirit of rugged individualism.

2

ARE YOU A SHEEP
OR A WOLF?

There are two types of people who stand out in the United States today: sheep and wolves. Sheep stay in their herd and follow their shepherd without questioning where he is leading them. Sheep trust that the shepherd looks out for their safety. Sheep believe that the shepherd would never do anything to cause them harm, that he only wants to protect them from the dangers of the world that lie outside the safety of his herd.

Wolves, on the other hand, do not aimlessly follow a shepherd. In the darkness of night, wolves howl, alerting the shepherd to their presence. Wolves are the people who do not passively accept the rules and direction of the shepherd without questioning his decisions. Wolves question the shepherd and act in a way that forces the shepherd also to question his decisions. Wolves challenge government regulations, reject government assistance, and demand that the government recognize and protect their natural rights. They are rugged individualists.

Unfortunately, the majority of Americans are sheep.

If you have not been able to figure this out, the sheep in this analogy are the millions of American citizens blindly following all levels of the government. The wolves are the people and groups within America that continuously question and challenge the decisions of the government. The wolves try to ensure that government does not overstep its constitutional limits and infringe on the American people's basic freedoms, which are ours by virtue of being human.

A large flock of Americans are passively allowing the government to infringe on their liberties in the name of safety. The federal government in general, and the president of the United States in particular, is using fear as a means to strip the American people of their rights.

Without hesitation, reticence, or skepticism, many Americans accept the government's contention that "freedom is not free." They believe the American Dream is in danger and are willing to surrender their fundamental freedoms to protect it. They are convinced that relinquishing a few rights here and a few liberties there will help the government to protect us better from evil terrorists bent on destroying the American way of life. How else can you explain the lack of outrage regarding the National Security Agency's having access to our telephone records, e-mails, financial documents, credit card numbers, medical records, and mail? How else can you account for the sheeplike acquiescence to unwarranted surveillance of public gatherings by police departments, random bag searches on subways and buses, and cameras on nearly every street corner? Back when people actually cared about protecting our constitutional rights, these things would have appalled them. But, alas, people are too busy panicking about terrorism to pay very much attention to reality—too busy being sheep.

The federal government has used fearmongering as a tactic to seduce the sheep into compliance with its unconstitutional laws; and it has worked! We should be smarter than to fall for these tactics that have failed in the past. Historical and modern-day examples show that relinquishing our liberties does not bring about a safer society. In fact, it shows the exact opposite. If we look to Israel and England and how they handle terrorism, we see that taking away liberties does not stop terrorist attacks. In fact, it emboldens terrorists.

> **The federal government has used fearmongering as a tactic to seduce the sheep into compliance with its unconstitutional laws; and it has worked!**

In Israel, it is a crime to be a member of various groups that have been labeled terrorist organizations. If you are suspected of membership, you are interrogated without being able to communicate with the outside world (which is unconstitutional in the United States, but has happened at the U.S. naval bases at Guantánamo Bay, Cuba, and in a military brig in South Carolina), and torture is likely to be used during the interrogations. However, today Israel is the continuous target of the most potent terrorist groups. Some people theorize that Israel's extreme tactics have provoked more extreme responses from the terrorists. Hence, the Israel-terrorist cycle continues.

If we look to the British government and how it handled the Irish Republican Army, it is clear that stripping citizens of their liberties in order to ensure their safety did not end the violence. Open discussion and peace talks did!

Even as recently as June 2007, England has been subject to attempted terrorist attacks. Two car bombs were found in central London, and a Jeep Cherokee carrying gas canisters was driven into Glasgow's International Airport. Thankfully, the plots of these madmen did not go according to plan, but Britain's strict terror laws—including the ability to hold a suspect for twenty-eight days in confinement without charge, and the use of more than four million surveillance cameras—did not and do not prevent terrorist attacks (though those cameras did aid in identifying the terrorists).

In 1927, Supreme Court Justice Louis D. Brandeis warned his colleagues against sanctioning the trade of liberty for security because of fear. Justice Brandeis noted that the Founding Fathers of this great nation valued liberty as both an end and a means. They believed that order cannot be secured through fear, "that fear breeds repression; that repression breeds hate; that hate menaces stable government; that the path of safety lies in the opportunity to discuss freely supposed grievances and proposed remedies. They believed in the power of reason as applied through public discussion."[1]

But in Israel, England, and the United States, the sheep conform to the government's demands *without* questioning what rights and liberties they are losing, or have lost, in order to protect them better from the unimaginable dangers of the outside world. The sheep may be afraid of terrorists, but they inexplicably follow their shepherd and stay with the herd. The wolves are afraid of terrorists, but they are not afraid of fear. They want security, but they want freedom more.

> The wolves are afraid of terrorists, but they are not afraid of fear. They want security, but they want freedom more.

THE POWER OF ONE!

All it took was one deranged man for Americans, and, for that matter, any person who flies, not to question having to take their wristwatches, belts, blazers, religious medals, and shoes off in an airport. That deranged man was Richard Reid, also known as the "Shoe Bomber." After Reid's failed attempt to blow up his shoe on an

American Airlines flight from Paris to Miami in 2001, taking your shoes and anything remotely metal off to have them X-rayed at an airport has become standard operating procedure. The sheep do not question that they are being forced to walk barefoot through metal detectors because of one man's failed attempt at using his shoe as a bomb. They simply do as they are told and follow the rest of the herd.[2]

If the government's police are not inspecting your shoes, they are rifling through your bags. The New York Police Department, along with many other police departments across the country, now conducts random bag searches in the subway, without suspicion or warrant, in order to prevent terrorist attacks. These random searches clearly violate the Fourth Amendment, which is meant to protect all persons from warrantless searches and seizures. If you are unlucky enough to be selected "randomly," the officers will stop you as you hurry to catch your morning train. As the doors slide closed on the platform below and your train departs, you stand helplessly as the bored cops search your bag.

In August 2005, a half-dozen New Yorkers filed a lawsuit to prevent the NYPD from violating the Fourth Amendment's guaranteed protection against warrantless invasions of your privacy. The plaintiffs charged that the NYPD violated the rights of thousands of innocent people, *all without any suspicion of wrongdoing*, by searching their purses, handbags, briefcases, and backpacks.[3]

Once, federal judges were wolves. After all, they are tenured for life; immune from the ebb and flow of politics; equal in power to the president and Congress. Sadly, not all judges behave as if this were still the case. In August 2006, Judge Chester Straub of the United States Court of Appeals for the Second Circuit ruled that the NYPD acted within the law because the subway bag searches fell within the "special needs exception" to the Fourth Amendment due to imminent terrorist threats. The court ruled that since the bag searches were distinct from a regular criminal investigation, bag searches on the New York subway somehow became completely legal, even though the Constitution says otherwise.[4] There is no "special needs" exception in the Fourth Amendment. The court simply made it up.

When Jefferson and his colleagues wrote the Bill of Rights, which includes the Fourth Amendment, they conspicuously omitted a "special needs exception." There is no value whatsoever to a guaranteed right (the right to be free from warrantless searches and seizures conducted by agents of the government) if the guarantee and the right disappear wherever the government's needs are "special."

The government will always argue that its needs are "special." The Constitution requires probable cause, an amount of evidence to persuade a judge that it is more likely than not that the person or thing to be searched possesses or contains evidence of a crime. The Constitution does not permit prophylactic searches, no matter what the cause or reason. Only sheep tolerate random searches.

In our nation's infancy, our Founding Fathers had the keen foresight to ensure that we would become a nation of wolves. When the United States was still just a British colony, trade was heavily regulated in order to benefit the motherland. These restrictions put significant economic strain on Britain's colonies, forcing them to smuggle essential goods in order to maintain reasonable prices. The smugglers outraged the Parliament, and Parliament gave

> There is no value whatsoever to a guaranteed right if the guarantee and the right disappear wherever the government's needs are "special." The government will always argue that its needs are "special."

soldiers nearly unlimited power to search any location in order to stop the smuggling. Parliament actually gave the soldiers and officers permission to use self-written search warrants, called *writs of assistance*, which enabled the soldiers and government agents to enter any private building or dwelling and search for whatever they had *authorized themselves to search for.*

Our Founding Fathers saw these atrocities and did not want the citizens of our new nation to emerge as sheep; they envisioned wolves, rugged individualists, hence, the Fourth Amendment to the Constitution, which prohibits warrantless searches and seizures of property.

Unfortunately, today our Founding Fathers are likely rolling in their graves as the Fourth Amendment has been completely ignored. National Security Letters (which will be discussed in Chapter 8), are now the modern-day writs of assistance. The wolves that the founders envisioned have regressed into sheep who succumb to random bag searches in public places due to the government's "special" needs.

In the cases that we have just touched upon, including intrusive and embarrassing (and frequently fruitless) airport searches, and privacy-invading, blatantly unconstitutional (and equally fruitless) bag searches, the government affirmed that it had the power to disregard the natural right to privacy. No referenda were taken and no legislature voted to employ these measures. Rather, unelected, faceless bureaucrats ordered us to act like sheep, and formerly courageous judges let them get away with it.

RELINQUISHING OUR RIGHT TO PRIVACY

By enacting the Patriot Act (known formally as the Uniting and Strengthening America by Providing Appropriate Tools Required to

Intercept and Obstruct Terrorism Act) in 2001, Congress has purported to give the president and his agents permission to listen to people's phone calls, read their e-mails, and obtain other personal information. Americans should be hyperaware of the plethora of personal information the government freely acquires from private citizens on a continuous basis. The ability of government agents to write their own search warrants, called National Security Letters (NSLs), gives federal agents access to any personal information a private company collects, without any kind of judicial approval. The private company, such as an HMO, a telephone company, a computer server, even a supermarket chain, is forbidden from telling its customer of the personal information it gave to the FBI. The company would be breaking the law if it told you, its loyal customer, that the FBI was requesting information and investigating you!

The most alarming part about the government's information gathering is the cooperation it receives from private industry. Currently, several corporations that cater to the general public obtain very private information from patrons without them even thinking twice.

If you want to go to Disney World, you will not be allowed to enter the park without giving up one of the most unique things about yourself: Your fingerprint! As if in anticipation of receiving a self-written search warrant from an FBI agent, Disney has been obtaining its visitors' fingerprints for years. According to Disney Parks public relations department, the policy was implemented in order to prevent customers from selling multiple-use passes to others and generally prevent fraud. Disney claims that the machine into which you must put your hand before entering merely measures various points on your finger, creating a mathematical calculation to match the pass to the patron, so calling it a fingerprint "is a little bit of a stretch!"[5] My editor experienced this at Sea World in the summer of 2007. Park personnel told her, "We're not taking your fingerprint; we're just taking a few measurements." Scary stuff.

> **If you want to go to Disney World, you will not be allowed to enter the park without giving up one of the most unique things about yourself: your fingerprint!**

How much personal information are the American people willing to give up for the sake of convenience? Sure, Disney is not the government, but with FBI agents able to write their own search warrants on a whim, what is stopping them from taking this information from Disney without you ever knowing? Should the American people really trust Disney and the U.S. government with uniquely personal and highly private data? Your fingerprint can get you into the theme park faster, but is surrendering your privacy really worth the cost of the government's being able to obtain your fingerprints with a self-written search warrant issued by any FBI agent, without you ever knowing about it?

Imagine if the sheep of the American flock ever became wolves. It would be astonishing to see how fast Disney would change its fingerprinting method if the wolves refused to give away such vital personal information and, therefore, did not enter the park. The sheep of the country do not realize how loud they could sound if they banded together and voiced their displeasure with their shepherds. If they did, they would have a much greater effect than the lone wolf howling in the night. They might even get Disney to change its practices, especially if their voices were loud enough to hurt Disney's bottom line.

Busch Gardens and Water Country USA were not satisfied with a mere fingerprint and have one-upped Disney. These two theme parks have implemented a HandEScan. Yes, it is exactly what you think. You put your hand into a machine, and it measures the top of your hand, takes your finger height, assesses your knuckle shape, and calculates the distance between the joints on your hands! The machine takes two separate images and then combines them for a full 3-D effect. What is the purpose of the HandEScan other than collecting valuable private information?

What about the tools available to everyone to spy via the Internet? Google's new Street View allows its users to look at practically any location around the world and see real, live people and their personal belongings! In fact, new Web sites are springing up almost daily with the sole purpose of using Street View to catch folks in compromising positions. Some images include people urinating on the side of the street, others walking into adult bookstores, and still others being pulled over by the police. Shouldn't the American people be terrified by this technology instead of fascinated with it? And shouldn't they do something about it?

The United States and its government officials are hypocrites. On one hand, the government has the ability to use NSLs to obtain any information that it could possibly desire. On the other hand, the United States has incredibly complicated privacy laws in place to protect citizens' personal lives from becoming public knowledge. But since Disney, Busch Gardens, Water Country USA, and Google are now effectively the government's agents, they will never be prosecuted, because they complied with the government's demands: They gather private information about you *for the government.* Maybe the government's abuse of NSLs will be exposed—that is, if the government doesn't declare this information a "state secret."

GPS technology will eventually allow the phone companies to

locate anyone, anywhere, at any time (and, as we will see in later chapters, the phone companies are all too willing to cooperate with the government). Instead of racing out to upgrade, we should be resisting this invasion of privacy!

Imagine that the FBI wants to know more about you because you just happened to call your cousin who is studying abroad in, say, Nairobi. This one phone call raises a red flag within the NSA wiretapping database. Due to one simple call, any FBI agent can write his own search warrant not only to your cell phone provider, but to any company you associate with, in any capacity. The agent, who could be a saint or a rogue, will know everything about you. The amount of your last annual bonus? THEY KNOW! Your company password to log in at work? THEY KNOW! The ATM fee you accepted at your local corner deli? THEY KNOW! That attractive new coworker you Googled? THEY KNOW (and could give you her phone number)! Afraid of pain, so you go to the new sedation dentist in town? THEY KNOW! Lactose intolerant? THEY KNOW (because you use your credit card to pay for your groceries and prescriptions)! Didn't make your high school varsity basketball team? THEY KNOW! Sent a Christmas package to Grandma marked "fragile"? THEY KNOW! Late returning a library book in college? THEY KNOW! Just sped through a yellow light? THEY KNOW (and have the picture to prove it)! They will know whom you are contacting and who is contacting you, and precisely where you are located at any point at any time. If you went to Disney, you can be sure they now have your fingerprint on file. And if you had a mole removed from your back and it came back as possibly cancerous, they know that too! They have more information about you stored digitally than you probably have stored about yourself!

MASS ARRESTS OF PEACEFUL PROTESTERS

As often as the government tries to conceal the information it seeks to obtain about innocent Americans, there are plenty of examples of the government gathering information out in public for all to see. In 2004, during the Republican National Convention (RNC) in New York City, the NYPD blatantly violated hundreds of people's rights by conducting surveillance and creating files on innocent persons who had no apparent intentions of breaking the law. Yes, that is what the files actually indicate—that these persons had no apparent intentions of breaking the law—and yet their actions were chronicled by the NYPD's RNC Intelligence Squad.

During the weeklong RNC, the NYPD arrested on minor offenses more than eighteen hundred protestors, who were held for up to two days in a dilapidated bus depot on a pier. These offenses are usually dealt with by issuing a simple summons, not by arresting people and obtaining their fingerprints. However, the City's Law Department tried to justify its military-like actions by claiming that "the preconvention intelligence justified detaining them all for fingerprinting."[6]

Where is the public outrage over these mass arrests? The protesters who were arrested are still fighting their charges. They are average Americans. Have Americans become so selfish that they don't care when the government blatantly violates somebody else's constitutional rights, as long as their own rights have not been violated? If the cops arrested your neighbor in July 2004 because they *thought* that he might be *thinking* about disrupting the RNC, is there any limit to what the cops will arrest your son or daughter for tomorrow?

Innocent Americans were arrested for protesting and speaking out against issues and policies that they were not satisfied with. These are the rights every American is guaranteed in the Constitution, in the First Amendment, in the Bill of Rights. It is the right of the people peaceably to assemble and petition the government for a redress of grievances. This is America, a democracy, not a dictatorship, in which you are forbidden to speak out against a tyrannical dictator!

> **This is America, a democracy, not a dictatorship, in which you are forbidden to speak out against a tyrannical dictator!**

During the RNC, one protester, Joshua Kinberg, was particularly targeted by the NYPD. Joshua was simply giving an interview to Ron Reagan on MSNBC's *Hardball* when he was arrested. He was not even protesting at the time he was cuffed and taken into custody.

In 2004, Joshua was a graduate student at the Parsons School of Design. For his master's thesis, Joshua, an imaginative young man, created a "wireless bicycle." The bike had all sorts of modern technology attached to it, including a cell phone and a laptop, along with tubes that could spray messages he received via the Internet onto the streets and sidewalks.

The spray used a chalk solution that washed away with rain water. Joshua intentionally used water-soluble chalk in order to avoid criminal mischief charges associated with creating graffiti. Even the cops who surveilled him admitted this in the NYPD's intelligence report.

Joshua sounds like an innovative kid on the path to accomplishing great things in this country, right? Not according to the NYPD. The four-page intelligence report on Joshua and his bicycle revealed extraordinary government paranoia. It seems that the NYPD was concerned that the bicycle was "capable of transferring activist-based messages on[to] the streets and sidewalks."[7] The file further supported the case against Joshua by reporting, "This bicycle, having been built for the sole purpose of protesting during the R.N.C., is capable of spraying anti-R.N.C.-type messages on surrounding streets and sidewalks, also supplying the rider with a quick vehicle of escape."[8]

When did it become a crime to write with chalk on the city streets and sidewalks? Has the NYPD arrested little children for doing it? No they have not. In fact, in 2001 there was a case in federal court in New York, *Lederman v. Giuliani*, that decided that using chalk on the city sidewalks is a traditional and constitutionally protected form of protest unique to New York.

Robert Lederman was the president of Artists' Response to Illegal State Tactics (ARTIST) and was arrested after he wrote, "Giuliani = Police State" and "God Bless America" on the sidewalk in front of police barricades. The court ruled that Lederman's First Amendment rights were violated when he was arrested for writing in chalk on the sidewalk. The court also stated that Lederman was unfairly targeted because of what he was writing, which suggested a "policy of selective enforcement which has created favored and unfavored categories of speakers which violates the Fourteenth Amendment and the New York State Constitution."[9]

Joshua Kinberg was unfairly targeted, just as Robert Lederman was, for writing in chalk. The kicker is that at the time of Joshua's arrest, he had not even used his "wireless bicycle" to write on the sidewalks or streets that day.

Kinberg was arrested as he was being interviewed while the MSNBC cameras were still rolling. As they cuffed Joshua, NYPD officers told the cameras that Joshua was being arrested for defacing the sidewalk. The footage, however, clearly showed that the NYPD had never seen Joshua deface anything. In fact, the police pulled up in the midst of the interview, during which Joshua did not demonstrate the bike or use it to write anything. When the NYPD arrived, the chalk was already on the sidewalk; there was no evidence that the chalk was Joshua's work. Ron Reagan even told the NYPD that the writing was on the sidewalk when he and Joshua arrived for the interview. It was impossible for the NYPD to have seen Joshua deface the sidewalk. Yet the NYPD lied—and did it with ease—and arrested a young man it knew was innocent of the charges in the summons that he received.

The scariest part of this attack on free speech is that most Americans have never heard of Joshua Kinberg, or Robert Lederman, and perhaps you hadn't either, until now. The American people should rally around them and realize how many of their constitutional rights are in jeopardy, but they don't. Could it be because they are all sheepish followers, and Joshua and Robert are wolves? Their cases bring attention to the erosion of constitutional rights. If they can get away with this with students, they can go after anyone. Unfortunately, the rest of the country is just following, like sheep, rather than leading, like wolves.

THERE ARE SOME WOLVES AMONG US

After September 11th many things changed throughout the United States. These changes were especially felt in New York City. Following the terrorist attacks, the NYPD's surveillance practices expanded exponentially.

In 2003, in Manhattan, federal Judge Charles S. Haight Jr. allowed the NYPD to have vast authority in order to investigate different religious, political, and social groups within the city. Not surprisingly, the NYPD took advantage of Judge Haight's loose guidelines, such as making mass arrests at the 2004 RNC. Not only did the NYPD videotape various events in which terrorist activity was highly unlikely, but even when they had good reasons to videotape events, they failed to apply for permission.

After the NYPD videotaped a march in Harlem and a demonstration in front of Mayor Bloomberg's home by the homeless, both of which tapings violated Judge Haight's 2003 guidelines, another lawsuit was filed. In a rare, refreshing display, Judge Haight acknowledged his fault and claimed responsibility for his loosely worded decision in 2003, stating that his words had not been "a model of clarity." In Judge Haight's most recent ruling on February 15th 2007, he set much stricter guidelines and penalties for the NYPD. More importantly, his ruling sent the message that if New York City cops trump civil liberties for the sake of establishing security, they will pay for it.[10] But don't hold your breath waiting for this to happen.

FOLLOWING THE HERD

The American flock continues to graze happily upon its safe, green grass within the bubble of the American Dream. The members of the flock are so satisfied with their tasty green morsels that they never take a break from their daily routine to look at the world around them. If the sheep would just pause from their grazing to wonder why they always graze in the same protected field and why they can't run free throughout all of the pastures, then maybe they would challenge their shepherds. But they don't, because they trust their shepherds with their entire existence and never question where they are leading the flock or, even more importantly, the pastures and freedom the shepherds have led them away from.

It is quite astonishing to look back in history and see how far we have regressed compared to what our Founding Fathers had envisioned for the United States. They designed the Bill of Rights to *guarantee* that the government would not interfere with individual, God-given rights. The *people* empowered the *government*, not the other way round.

Yet the government has steadily been taking away the rights guaranteed to all Americans in the Constitution. Sadly, our country is deteriorating into the same lack-of-liberties state our Founding Fathers fought and worked so hard to avoid. Their goal was to differentiate us from Britain by establishing a limited government, circumscribed by a written Constitution, which was to be inviolable: The Supreme Law of the Land. Even though they succeeded, and over time the brilliance of the Constitution remains, its impact has dissipated.

In the following chapters, we will take a brief trip back in time and see how we really are becoming the country we nobly seceded from in 1776.

3

A HISTORY OF ABUSE

The marriage of government suppression of liberty and the sheepishness of Americans is not a new development. In fact, since the Constitution was drafted, the United States government has been abusing its power and trying to undermine freedom.

As the eighteenth century wound to a close, the United States was quickly approaching a state of war with France, after we won our revolution. The French were suspicious of Anglo-American relations, being at war with Britain themselves; American support of the French Revolution did little to ease the tension; and we were failing in our attempts at diplomacy with France. The two major political parties in America, the Federalists and the Anti-Federalists (also called the Republicans), clashed over what route to take in relations with France. By 1798, the United States and France were at war, though unofficially so, and the Federalist government took steps to silence both the French and the Anti-Federalists.

The Federalists painted the Anti-Federalists as a "French faction," while Jefferson's Anti-Federalists embraced the ideals of liberty and equality espoused in the French Revolution. Federalist politicians seized upon the anti-French sentiment of the day, comparing the anticipated fall of the Anti-Federalists to the descent of Lucifer.

> Federalist politicians seized upon the anti-French sentiment of the day, comparing the anticipated fall of the Anti-Federalists to the descent of Lucifer.

The Federalist-controlled Congress enacted legislation allegedly in response to the hostile actions of the French Revolutionary government, but actually designed to destroy Thomas Jefferson's Anti-Federalists. The very name of the statutes would equate for centuries, even into the present day, with American governmental tyranny: The Alien and Sedition Acts.

The Alien and Sedition Acts consisted of three laws: the *Alien Friends Act*, the *Alien Enemies Act*, and the *Sedition Act*. The first two acts were designed to permit the arrest and deportation of foreign nationals of countries with which the United States was at war or with which war loomed. Not a single foreign national was ever apprehended or deported under either of the Alien Acts.

The Sedition Act punished the printing, publishing, or uttering of any "false, scandalous and malicious . . . writings against the United States, or either house of Congress . . . or the President."[1] If any of these prohibited "malicious writings" possessed the requisite "intent to defame the[m] . . . or to bring them . . . into contempt or disrepute . . . or to excite against them . . . the hatred of the good people of the United States," the speaker or writer could be prosecuted. Thus, the Sedition Act proscribed speaking ill of President Adams and the Federalist Congress, but left the door open to criticism of Vice President Jefferson, the Acts' chief detractor. Under such a system, the Federalists could enjoy the benefits of holding public office without the annoyances and hindrances that fault-finding opposition tends to provide. Imagine that: we just embraced the Declaration of Independence against a tyrant, won a Revolution from him, enacted a Constitution so no tyrant could ever reign here, and one of the first matters addressed by the new Federalist government was to make criticism of it criminal! It's amazing how consistent human nature is, isn't it? Things haven't changed much.

The Federalists saw the Sedition Act as a means to protect the government by safeguarding it against dangerous opinions. The Sedition Act also served to acknowledge that prison and financial penalties would solve political controversies, instead of open debate and free flow of ideas and opinions.

One of the earliest prosecutions under the Sedition Act was also one of the most memorable. Matthew Lyon, a member of Congress, a Jeffersonian, and a critic of the Adams Administration, brought tabloid dramatics to the floor of the House of Representatives when he spat in the face of a Federalist member of Congress. This move prompted a duel, as Lyon attacked with a pair of fire tongs and the Federalist defended himself wildly with his cane. After the men were removed from the building, the fighting resumed outside.

Lyon did not stop there. Stirring up further controversy, he openly bashed the Adams Administration, announcing that under Adams, "every consideration of public welfare was swallowed up in a continual grasp for power, in an unbounded thirst for ridiculous pomp, foolish adoration, and selfish avarice." Although Lyon's statements were hardly defamatory, he was charged, tried, and

> **Matthew Lyon brought tabloid dramatics to the floor of the House of Representatives when he spat in the face of a Federalist member of Congress. This move prompted a duel, as Lyon attacked with a pair of fire tongs and the Federalist defended himself wildly with his cane.**

convicted for violating the Sedition Act. He received a four-month prison term.

After his inauguration, President Jefferson pardoned everyone convicted under the Sedition Act, and he allowed the Alien and Sedition Acts to expire while he was in office. Jefferson later pushed local officials to retaliate against Federalist editors, and, although convictions resulted, the level of persecution was scant in comparison to the widespread suppression that took place under the Sedition Act. Forty years later, Congress decided to reimburse people for fines they paid as a result of convictions under the Sedition Act.

> **During the Civil War, Lincoln closed newspapers across the country and seized telegraph lines so as to censor communications that he perceived as threats to his war efforts.**

But the progress made by Jefferson receded once President Lincoln took office. During the Civil War, Lincoln closed newspapers across the country and seized telegraph lines so as to censor communications that he perceived as threats to his war efforts. He shut down the *Chicago Times*, and even had one newspaper editor banished from Ohio! Strangely, at the time, Americans viewed banishment as a punishment that allowed criminals to save face.

In the case of Clement Vallandigham, however, the president showed a disregard for the natural law and a lust for power rare even in American history. Vallandigham, a congressman from Dayton, Ohio, refused to watch idly as basic freedoms dissolved under Lincoln. He openly condemned Lincoln's military arrests of civilians, his suspension of habeas corpus, and his persecution of dissenting opinions. Vallandigham also called for Lincoln's impeachment for the president's blatant and repeated violations of the Constitution.

The Ohio Legislature fired the first volley in the battle to quiet Vallandigham. Republicans there redrew, or "gerrymandered," the lines of Vallandigham's congressional district to drive him out of Congress. Sure enough, in 1862, Vallandigham, who ran on a platform of opposition to Abraham Lincoln, lost his seat in the Congress after nearly twenty years of service there.

Although no longer a member of Congress, Vallandigham loved the public eye and ear, and consistently sought them out as he voiced his disapproval of the war and President Lincoln through public speeches. Even though Vallandigham was displeased with the government and opposed the war, he was firm in respecting the law and the Constitution. In a speech delivered in Dayton, Ohio, on August 2nd 1862, while still a member of Congress, Vallandigham told the crowd, "No matter how distasteful constitutions and laws may be, they must be obeyed. I am opposed to all mobs, and opposed also . . . to all violations of [the C]onstitution and law[s] by men in authority—public servants. The danger from usurpations and violations by them is fifty-fold greater than from any other quarter, because these violations and usurpations come clothed with [a] false semblance of authority."[2]

Vallandigham hit the nail on the head here. The men and women of the federal government are the guardians of the Constitution, and they violate their duty and our trust in them when they diminish and abridge the rights of

> The men and women of the federal government are the guardians of the Constitution, and they violate their duty and our trust in them when they diminish and abridge the rights of the people they serve.

the people they serve; and the damage they cause is "fifty-fold" more harmful than ordinary crimes, because when the government breaks the law, it does so with a false semblance of authority; and it does it again and again and again.

By May 5th 1863, Lincoln, who believed that he could suppress the speech he feared and hated, took a cue from President Adams's prosecution of Congressman Lyon, ordered Union General Ambrose Burnside to use troops to break into former Congressman Vallandigham's home (through at least two doors), arrest him, and bring him to Cincinnati for trial. Some of Vallandigham's supporters rang the town fire bells and attempted to gather a group of people to rescue their hero, but their efforts failed.

The former member of Congress was held without bail in a military prison in Cincinnati. Vallandigham wrote a letter to the "Democracy of Ohio" from prison, in which he fiercely defended his actions. The letter stated, "I am here in a military bastille for no other offence than my political opinions and the defense of them, and of the rights of the people, and of your Constitutional liberties."[3] Those liberties were once again in serious jeopardy, as Vallandigham faced a difficult battle for his freedom against a president who openly rejected his oath to uphold the Constitution.

One of President Lincoln's particularly offensive abuses of the Constitution was his suspension of the writ of habeas corpus. This legal term refers to a prisoner's right to compel his jailer to allow him to go before a judge, and to justify legally his confinement. If no lawful charges have been brought against him, the prisoner is released. Habeas corpus is an ancient right recognized by Anglo-American law since 1215. The Constitution itself recognizes this right and prohibits its suspension except by Congress and only in the case of invasion or rebellion—violence so horrific that the courts are unable to sit and adjudicate prisoners' rights.

Vallandigham, in keeping with his fight against Lincoln's suspension of habeas corpus, petitioned a federal court in Ohio for his release, as he was not in the military or naval service and thus not subject to the military authority that arrested him and was about to put the former congressman on trial. Judge Humphrey Leavitt firmly rejected Vallandigham's petition, looking to the government as a whole so as to justify Vallandigham's illicit detention. Leavitt supported his ruling, writing: "Self-preservation is a paramount law, which a nation, as well as an individual, may find it necessary to invoke."[4] Leavitt got it wrong; the government does not triumph over the individual liberties guaranteed by the Constitution.

Clement Vallandigham was tried before a military commission appointed by General Burnside and was, not surprisingly, quickly convicted. The military commission sentenced Vallandigham to life imprisonment, but Lincoln took the liberty of altering the sentence and banished Vallandigham to the Confederacy. In reflecting upon the punishment meted out to the former representative, Lincoln asked, "Must I shoot a simple-minded soldier boy who deserts, and not touch a hair of the wily agitator who induces him to desert?"[5]

Lincoln had a gift for clever, pithy, catchy phrases that could embody his philosophy of government in a way that the common person could understand and accept. Unfortunately for the Great Perverter of the Constitution, he was almost always expressing a view directly at odds with the Constitution that he swore (in an oath "registered in Heaven," as he was fond of saying) to uphold. That Constitution, which is the sole source of all presidential power, gave him neither the right to "shoot a simple-minded [American] soldier boy" nor the right to impair in any way "the wily agitator" using his First Amendment protected rights.

> Unfortunately for the Great Perverter of the Constitution, he was almost always expressing a view directly at odds with the Constitution that he swore (in an oath "registered in Heaven," as he was fond of saying) to uphold.

Although the case of Vallandigham is a stain on the history of American freedom, the reaction to his unconstitutional, unlawful, and unnatural arrest demonstrated the awareness that Americans in the 1860s had of the loss of freedom and their willingness to be wolves about it. Immediately following Vallandigham's arrest, the citizens of Dayton rioted and burned the local Republican newspaper building, cut down telegraph lines, and destroyed a bridge. General Burnside declared martial law in Dayton and was forced to send troops to the Ohio town to restore order. The army also "suppressed" the *Empire*, a newspaper that supported Vallandigham. The damages resulting from the riots totaled $39,000, which would be close to $1,000,000 today.[6] Order was restored, but the divide over the Vallandigham arrest was gripping the country.

Support grew for Vallandigham in the coming days; more than three thousand people gathered in Union Square in New York City to protest his arrest and jailing. New York Republican Governor Horatio Seymour sent a letter to the Vallandigham supporters in Albany, in which he wrote, "Having given [the Lincoln Administration] a generous support in the conduct of the war, we pause to see what kind of a government it is for which we are asked to pour out our blood and our treasure. The action of the Administration will determine . . . whether this war is waged to put down rebellion [in] the South, or destroy free institutions [in] the North."[7] In May 1863, one newspaper vilified Governor Seymour's efforts: The *New York Times* referred to his words as "the lowest manifestation we have ever seen of the low patriotism of certain classes of politicians."[8] So the *New York Times* backed a Republican president who exercised powers never granted to him by the Constitution, and who suppressed and punished the speech that he feared and hated. Oh, how the times have changed (no pun intended)!

The *Times* and the newspapers that attacked Governor Seymour stood by the Lincoln Administration like sheep, fearful of being separated from the herd and abandoned. They watched as President Lincoln closed newspapers across the country and preferred to speak as they were told, rather than in defiance of a tyrant, or not at all. If not for wolves like Governor Seymour and Congressman Vallandigham, our liberties would go unprotected and such transgressions would be forgotten.

Vallandigham stayed in the news after his banishment to the Confederacy. Virtually every move he made in the South was front page news in the *New York Times*. At the 1863 Ohio Democratic State Convention, Vallandigham was nominated to run for governor, even though he didn't live in Ohio, receiving over 97 percent of votes from the delegates. The party members at the convention also adopted resolutions insisting that President Lincoln respect freedom of speech and freedom of the press. Vallandigham never held office again.

The list of resolutions drafted by Vallandigham's supporters in Albany, referred to as the "Albany Resolves," were sent to President Lincoln, and the president actually responded to the complaints in a widely published letter. In the letter, Lincoln defended his suspensions of civil liberties by claiming they were entirely necessary in the name of public safety, and that he waited as long as possible to suspend those liberties. In referring to Vallandigham's arrest and trial, Lincoln claimed that Vallandigham's arrest was not made because of the fiery politician's criticism of the Lincoln Administration, but rather because "Mr. Vallandigham avows his hostility to the war on the part of the Union; and his arrest was made because he was laboring, with some effect, to prevent the raising of troops; to encourage desertions from the army; and to leave the rebellion without an adequate military force to suppress it."[9] Lincoln was arguing that, through his speeches, Vallandigham was wrecking the Union's war effort.

Lincoln had argued for the suspension of the writ of habeas corpus two years earlier, at a meeting of Congress in 1861 on the Fourth of July. He asked, "[A]re all the laws, but one, to go unexecuted, and the government itself go to pieces, lest that one be violated? Even in such a case, would not the official oath be broken, if the government should be overthrown, when it was believed that disregarding the single law, would tend to preserve it? But it was not believed that this question was presented. It was not believed that any law was violated. The provision of the Constitution that 'The privilege of the writ of habeas corpus, shall not be suspended unless when, in cases of rebellion or invasion, the public safety may require it,' is equivalent to a provision—is a provision—that such privilege may be suspended when, in cases of rebellion, or invasion, the public safety does require it. It was

> **Those frightened by war and conflict, the first to succumb to the erosion of our freedoms, are, like Lincoln, dead wrong. When all of our liberties are gone, there will be nothing left to protect.**

decided that we have a case of rebellion, and that the public safety does require the qualified suspension of the privilege of the writ which was authorized to be made."[10]

The thought that Lincoln expressed was a classic formulation of the argument against freedom, the argument that security and stability come at the expense of the laws and the freedoms that our Constitution was intended to guarantee. Those frightened by war and conflict, the first to succumb to the erosion of our freedoms, are, like Lincoln, dead wrong. When all of our liberties are gone, there will be nothing left to protect.

PATRIOTISM OR BLIND LOYALTY?

Despite the public outcry over government suppression of speech during the Civil War, things had not changed much in the United States even fifty years later, at the height of World War I. The courts had developed serious protection for freedom of speech, but apparently declined to exercise it in the case of Steven Wimmer, a U.S. citizen who had lived in Germany.

Wimmer essentially claimed that the German government was kinder to its citizens than the American government, and a federal grand jury charged him with a felony *for saying so*. The court that tried him ignored the Supreme Court's rule requiring that a "clear and present danger" exist before speech could be punished. The statements that were deemed felonious under the Espionage Act, passed on June 15th 1917, were "that America did not have a chance to win this war; that President Wilson started the war to protect the Wall Street brokers, who had purchased English and French securities; that President Wilson was a friend of the rich man; and that, when he [Wimmer] was in Germany about six years ago, he found that the Kaiser was always a friend of the poor man."[11] Wimmer appealed his conviction, but lost.[12]

Along with the advent of the twentieth century came the rise of anarchism. *Anarchism* is defined as "a political theory holding all forms of government to be unnecessary and undesirable and advocating a society based on voluntary cooperation and free association of individuals and groups."[13] Under anarchist principles, any form of government exploits and oppresses the people. One of the chosen methods of advancing the political aim of eliminating government was assassination. From 1894 to 1901, anarchists succeeded in knocking off four European leaders: President Sadi Carnot of France, King Humbert of Italy, Empress Elisabeth of Bavaria, and Spanish statesman Cánovas del Castillo.

Anarchism spread quickly among the poor and uneducated, providing a channel for their angst at working conditions and their life station. Leon Czolgosz was the ideal candidate to subscribe to anarchism: The son of Polish immigrants, Czolgosz had left school at an early age and had worked in various factory jobs ever since. He took a job in Cleveland in a wire mill and grew increasingly interested in socialism and anarchism.[14]

President William McKinley, the most popular president since Lincoln, visited the Pan-American Exposition in Buffalo, New York, on September 6th 1901. Buffalo and Cleveland are only 185 miles apart, and Czolgosz made the short train trip and waited two hours in eighty-two-degree heat to shake McKinley's hand. When the president reached to greet Czolgosz, the anarchist unloaded two rounds of his revolver into McKinley's chest. The twenty-fifth president of the United States died eight days later from wounds related to the bullets.[15]

In the wake of an anarchist slaying the president on New York soil, the New York Legislature enacted a criminal anarchy measure. Under the Criminal Anarchy Act of 1902, it was a felony to attempt to foster the violent overthrow of the government.[16] The text of the Act defined criminal anarchy as "the doctrine that organized government should be overthrown by force or violence, or by assassination of the executive head or of any of the executive officials of the government, or by any unlawful means."[17] Advocacy of anarchism "by word of mouth or writing"[18] would send you to Sing Sing for five to ten years.

Grouping communism (which desires tyrannical government) with anarchism (which desires no government), the New York Legislature decided to combat the "Red" threat and established on March 26th 1919, the Joint Legislative Committee to Investigate Seditious Activities. Senator Clayton R. Lusk of Cortland County headed the committee (commonly called the "Lusk Committee"), which had broad investigative powers to scrutinize individuals and groups suspected of advocating criminal anarchy. Senator J. Henry Walters, whose resolution created the Lusk Committee, was confident that the Lusk Committee would serve its purpose, declaring, "I trust that we shall not stop at anything or with anybody in our effort to tear Bolshevism up with the roots and hurl it into the sea."[19] As we shall shortly see, it didn't matter to the State of New York that getting rid of Bolshevism meant hurling free speech into the sea as well.

The Lusk Committee authorized a series of raids under the cover of darkness on Saturday, November 8th 1919. The two most prominent men snared were "Big Jim" Larkin, an "Irish agitator and strike leader," and Benjamin Gitlow, a former state assemblyman. Larkin and Gitlow, who were associated with a socialist newspaper titled the

Revolutionary Age, were held on $15,000 bail. The *Revolutionary Age* had printed official statements of the Communist Party and the Left Wing Socialist Party, two of the Lusk Committee's favorite targets.[20]

Gitlow challenged the constitutionality of the Criminal Anarchy Act, arguing that it violated his First Amendment-guaranteed right to freedom of speech. Both he and Larkin were convicted.

The Supreme Court upheld Gitlow's conviction. Even though the pamphlets that Gitlow published were printed in Yiddish and did not urge immediate overthrow of the government, and even though no demonstrable violence came about as a result of those almost-impossible-for-the-average-New-Yorker-to-read pamphlets, Justice Sanford found that "the immediate danger is none the less real and substantial, because the effect of a given utterance cannot be accurately foreseen."[21]

In holding that the New York Legislature had a right to promote public safety through its suppression of free speech, Sanford cautioned "that a single revolutionary spark may kindle into a fire that, smoldering for a time, may burst into a sweeping and destructive conflagration."[22]

So, what Thomas Paine and his colleagues did to the king of England in order to acquire a government that would protect free speech actually brought his descendants one that would banish free speech.

Justice Holmes attacked the reasoning of the Court and viewed the decision as a diversion from the "clear and present danger" test. He lamented that especially in the case of Benjamin Gitlow, "there was no present danger" to overthrow the United States government "on the part of the admittedly small minority who shared the defendant's views."

Holmes cautioned punishing speech such as Gitlow's "Left Wing Manifesto," in which the temporal link between words and action was too distant. In words that embrace democratic change through First Amendment freedoms, Justice Holmes wrote: "If . . . the beliefs expressed in proletarian dictatorship are destined to be accepted . . . the only meaning of free speech is that they should be given their chance and have their way."[23]

THE END OF FREEDOM AND
THE BEGINNING OF WWII

As questionable as the Wimmer, Larkin, and Gitlow convictions were, they were only a shadow of the atrocities that our government would commit during World War II. No liberty was safe at war; freedom of speech, due process, and fair trials went out the door as FDR (and later, Truman) turned the government's attention away from defending the Constitution.

The first War Powers Act, passed on December 18th 1941, increased FDR's executive authority and specifically provided him with the power to monitor and censor American international communications. On December 19th 1941, FDR signed Executive Order 8985, establishing the Office of Censorship.[24]

Not only did FDR monitor international communications, but he also established press codes, promulgated by the new Office of Censorship, to prevent any criticism of the national effort or foreign relations. Papers

> No liberty was safe at war; freedom of speech, due process, and fair trials went out the door as FDR (and later, Truman) turned the government's attention away from defending the Constitution.

throughout the United States complied with the press codes and seemed to put up little fight, if any.

The Supreme Court was also responsible for some of the lowest moments in the history of American freedom during World War II. Tragically, the Court's grievous errors cost U.S. citizens more than their right to criticism and to speak: they cost many people their literal freedom, and others, their lives.

Fear of Japanese spies and treasonous Japanese American citizens resulted in Executive Order 9066, requiring the internment of Japanese Americans during the war. Approximately 120,000 people were moved to internment camps, called "War Relocation Centers," in an effort to keep Japanese Americans away from the West Coast. Sixty-two percent of these people were American citizens, and many of them were born in the United States. The Relocation Centers, most of which were located on Native American reservations, consisted of simple barracks, without plumbing or cooking facilities. The barracks were surrounded by armed guards, and the residents (often families with small children) were given a food budget of forty-five cents per day. The government had stripped these citizens of their freedom and much of their property on an unconstitutional and racist whim.

One Japanese-American, Fred Korematsu, wanted to remain with his Italian American girlfriend and refused to cooperate. In a 6 to 3 decision, the Supreme Court upheld the constitutionality of FDR's order, finding that the danger posed by Japanese Americans outweighed the imposition on their rights. A Department of Justice official later said that the appearance of this danger was based on "wilful historical inaccuracies and intentional falsehoods."[25]

Attacking the racial basis of the internment program, Justice Frank Murphy dissented:

Racial discrimination in any form and in any degree has no justifiable part whatever in our democratic way of life. It is unattractive in any setting but it is utterly revolting among a free people who have embraced the principles set forth in the Constitution of the United States. All residents of this nation are kin in some way by blood or culture to a foreign land. Yet they are primarily and necessarily a part of the new and distinct civilization of the United States. They must accordingly be treated at all times as the heirs of the American experiment and as entitled to all the rights and freedoms guaranteed by the Constitution.[26]

It took more than thirty years before the government would apologize for its conduct and formally repeal the order. In 1976, President Gerald Ford issued presidential Proclamation 4417: "I call upon the American people to affirm with me this American Promise—that we have learned from the tragedy of that long-ago experience forever to treasure liberty and justice for each individual American, and resolve that this kind of action shall never again be repeated." In 1998, President Clinton honored Fred Korematsu with the Presidential Medal of Freedom, the highest civilian honor any American can ever hope to receive.

The Court persisted in its abominable disregard for civil rights when it faced a small band of Germans and German Americans charged with treason. Richard Quirin, along with seven fellow conspirators who had lived in the United States, learned military skills, such as how to build explosives and how to write in code, at a school for German saboteurs near Berlin. Upon returning to the United States, Quirin and the others traveled from New York to

Florida in a German submarine, in German military uniforms, plotting to destroy U.S. property and hinder the war effort.[27]

The plan was foiled when two of the saboteurs turned themselves in to the FBI. At first, the FBI refused to believe they were spies. But eventually the saboteurs convinced them, and the remaining conspirators were apprehended. All of them were sentenced before a military tribunal and held as unlawful combatants.

The Supreme Court upheld the president's use of a military tribunal and the decision to execute the Germans, sending six of the men to the electric chair on August 8th 1942. While the men were undeniably spies and a threat to be taken seriously, the trial itself was a farce—the defense attorney was only allowed to accept the assignment on the grounds that he would enter a guilty plea for the Germans. Heroically, defense attorney Kenneth Royall did not comply; rather, he stood up for the saboteurs' right to due process and a fair trial. As a recognition of Royall's courage, President Truman promoted him to brigadier general, and he was later named secretary of war.[28]

> Baseless accusations and secret evidence served to convict innocent Americans of crimes that they did not commit, as Communism spread inside and outside the United States and the "Red Scare" gripped the nation.

The fears that chilled constitutional rights and natural liberties during World War II peaked in the Cold War that followed. Baseless accusations and secret evidence served to convict innocent Americans of crimes that they did not commit, as Communism spread inside and outside the United States and the "Red Scare" gripped the nation.

President Truman signed Executive Order 9835 in 1947, establishing "Loyalty Boards" to review federal employees suspected of having ties to the Communist Party. A low-level employee of the Civil Service Commission in Washington, DC, Dorothy Bailey, was fired for supposed connections to the Communist Party. Although she submitted some seventy affidavits denying the allegations, and although no evidence was shown to her, the Supreme Court upheld the Loyalty Board's decision to discharge her. As U.S. Court of Appeals Judge Henry W. Edgerton wrote in dissent: "Without trial by jury, without evidence, and without even being allowed to confront her accusers or to know their identity, a citizen of the United States has been found disloyal to the government of the United States."[29]

As we will see in the chapters that follow, when we show the government that we will not protest its abuses of the natural law and will allow it to trample our freedoms just because there is a war being waged, we create an incentive for the government to go to war. Our complacency creates a perpetual cycle: The government wages wars in our names, and we relinquish more of our rights in the name of safety.

4

PEACETIME SPEECH SUPPRESSION

Suppression of our individual right to freedom of speech is not a relic of the past, nor does it seem likely to end in the near future. It has become a fact of everyday life for Americans; the sheep among us are herded and silent, while the very few wolves have curled their lips to reveal potent jaws. This chapter chronicles our decline in courage, beginning with the bloodcurdling howl of a wolf pack in Chicago.

THE HAYMARKET RIOTS

On Saturday, May 1st 1886, union workers marched through the streets of Chicago, protesting their long hours. The massive throng of eighty thousand men chanted in unison: "Eight hours for work, eight hours for rest, and eight hours for what we will!" The strike began as a peaceful demonstration, but the parade bordered on becoming a mob when the police fought with and killed several demonstrators. Little did the police realize—or care—that they were also making an assault on another vulnerable foe of the government: The First Amendment.

Union workers planned a protest in response to the deaths of their colleagues. The protest, organized by the Federation of Organized Trade and Labor Unions, was approved by Mayor Carter Harrison Sr. for May 4th. In the face of a violent wind and a driving rain, nearly twenty-five hundred men gathered to show support for the workers who had been brutally murdered over the weekend. As the weather conditions worsened, most of the men, along with Mayor Harrison, went home. But as the last demonstrator wound up his speech, the large police force assembled around the workers unleashed a surprise attack, killing four unsuspecting protestors in another round of bloodshed.

Evenly matched in numbers, one of the two hundred remaining workers launched a bomb at the police line, killing one officer and wounding others. The mob dispersed, and the police captured eight men and brought them to trial as the ringleaders of the tragic protest.

The man who threw the explosive into the police force was never identified. Yet the men whom the police finally arrested were charged with encouraging an unknown felon and inciting him to violence. The unfortunate eight faced murder charges and an incensed court. Seven of them received a death sentence. One of them decided to take matters into his own hands.

The Chicago Public Library, which has published a pamphlet on the Haymarket Riots, does not recognize the following grisly part of the story, but it has been reported elsewhere. According to some, Louis Lingg, one of the seven sentenced to death, managed to smuggle a piece of dynamite into his prison cell. The dynamite, shaped like a cigar, fit neatly into Lingg's mouth. As though he were about to enjoy casually a fine tobacco product, Lingg ignited the explosive in his mouth, blowing off half of his face and most of his lower jaw in a cloud of gore. Incredibly, Lingg did not die immediately, nor did he pass out. He maintained consciousness for hours, and as he lay dying in his dismal prison cell, he dipped his fingertips into his own blood and traced a final protest on the stone wall: "Long Live Anarchy."

Whether the men were anarchists or not, they proudly championed their right to free speech and refused to be cowed like sheep when the government beat them down. The wolves howled in Chicago that night, with an echo that carried far from the prison cells.

The day after Lingg committed suicide, four of the other union organizers were scheduled to be hanged. The executioners led them to the gallows, having clothed them in hooded white robes. The convicts kept their composure in the face of imminent death and sang "La Marseillaise," the song of the French revolutionaries who stood against a tyrannical government. They were courage personified, men with the hearts of wolves. One wonders if, as in the classic film *Casablanca*, the audience around the gallows began to sing with them, in support of the men whose courage had not faltered.

Just before falling to his death, one of the men is reported to have cried out a poignant prophecy: "The time will come when our silence will be more powerful than the voices you strangle today!"[1]

FREE SPEECH TODAY

Public school students and employees in both the private and public sectors (particularly government employees) have come into the spotlight for their speech, prompting court decisions that could have lasting implications for our own ability to speak freely. These cases are bizarre and sometimes absurd, but we ought to take them seriously if we are to understand and protect our unique privilege to express ourselves and to engage in public debate.

> As Louis Lingg lay dying in his dismal prison cell, he dipped his fingertips into his own blood and traced a final protest on the stone wall: "Long Live Anarchy."

Even in developed European countries such as England, Germany, and France, persons do not have all of the protections that are guaranteed here by the First Amendment. In many countries, circumscribed and particular exceptions to the right to speak freely prevent people from participating in free and open discussion of public issues. Comments pertaining to race or religion, for example, can easily result in criminal charges. Orhan Pamuk, a Turkish winner of the Nobel Prize for Literature, was charged with violating a law forbidding citizens to insult the Turkish government. Had Pamuk been convicted, he would have faced a prison sentence for his comments about the Armenians who were killed in Turkey in 1915. Pamuk was simply reciting an historical fact.

AN INTREPID IOWAN

In the United States, on the other hand, unpopular speech gets full protection by the courts and the Constitution, except in a few limited cases. The right to speak out in opposition to your government is one of the most fundamental rights that we have, and securing it was a major goal of our Revolutionary War.

One of the major free speech issues currently garnering attention in the U.S. media, the right of students to speak freely, traces back to a famous Supreme Court case in which a school suspended students for wearing armbands. In December 1965, a Des Moines, Iowa, junior high student, Mary Beth Tinker, argued in favor of her right to protest the Vietnam War by wearing a black armband. The Court determined that the black armband was a valid and protected expression under the First Amendment because her attire neither disrupted the school nor impinged upon any other student's rights.

THE FREDERICK FIASCO

Nearly forty years later, Joe Frederick, a student at Juneau-Douglas High School in Juneau, Alaska, drew attention to his own questionable speech at the 2002 Winter Olympics Torch Relay in Juneau. Just across the street from his school, Frederick held up a banner that read, "Bong Hits 4 Jesus" as the procession passed by him. He refused to take the sign down and was suspended by an irate principal, Deborah Morse. Frederick sued Morse, alleging a violation of his First Amendment rights, and the battle continued all the way to the Supreme Court.

If the school can prevent speech that it dislikes, such as comments that could be considered a promotion of illegal drug use, then the *Frederick* case would diminish the rule set down in *Tinker*. Not only was Frederick outside of the school, but he wasn't even on school property.

The court decided to take the school's side in a 5 to 4 decision protecting the principal's authority to discipline students for their speech. This authority comes at the cost of every student's right to speak freely. Their right to open debate is especially important, since adolescence and high school constitute a formative period during which our future lawyers, judges, and professionals develop their ways of thinking about issues that might affect *our* right to speak freely.

THE LITTLE WINNIE WAR

A student at Redwood Middle School in Napa, California, ran into similar difficulties over an even tamer exercise of her right to express herself. Toni Kay Scott decided that she was going to wear her Winnie the Pooh socks to school one day, only to find herself being dragged by a cop to the principal's office. The school would only allow solid-color clothing. Stripes or other aberrations could, according to the principal, lead to gang violence.

What sort of gang was Scott promoting? A group of vicious stuffed animals? Honey-eating hell-raisers? Although some restrictions on what students wear to class may be helpful in curbing gang violence, blanket restrictions, such as the one on patterns of any kind, violate the personal right of expression. They offend students' right to free speech, and they offend common sense.

In July 2007, Judge Raymond Guadagni of the Napa Superior Court ruled in favor of Toni Kay Scott's right to wear her Winnie the Pooh socks. Lawyers in of Northern California handled Scott's case and ended the Napa school's unconstitutional dress code.

> **What sort of gang was Scott promoting? A group of vicious stuffed animals? Honey-eating hell-raisers?**

ONLINE PROTECTION—OR OPPRESSION?

Volunteer lawyers recently defended your right to free speech in a New York case on Internet censorship: *ACLU v. Gonzales.* The Child Online Protection Act (COPA), enacted by Congress in 1998, loomed over the Internet, threatening online speech with criminal sanctions and fines of up to $50,000 per day for making available any material found to be "harmful to minors," regardless of its nature or utility for adults. COPA seriously threatened the free flow of ideas and information over the Internet; a discussion of safe sex, for example, might result in sanctions under the Act. Fortunately, the federal court that took the case recognized the effectiveness of Internet filters and parental control, which also protect children, without COPA-like sanctions or their chilling effect on free speech. It invalidated the COPA law.

But the government's infringement on the First Amendment doesn't stop at banning colorful socks and discussions about safe sex. Believe it or not, you can be arrested for reading the First Amendment itself.

"WELL, SHUT MY MOUTH!"

In July 2007, one of the many colorful characters in New York City's Union Square was Bill Talen, better known as Reverend Billy, decked out in a white suit and a bleached-blonde pompadour. Reverend Billy, who is not actually ordained, was in Union Square that day to educate the people of New York about the First Amendment. He was arrested by police while reciting the text through a bullhorn and charged with harassment of a public official.[2] The First Amendment doesn't even protect itself anymore!

> **The First Amendment doesn't even protect itself anymore!**

On April 22nd 2000, Doris Haddock, better known as "Granny D," was arrested in the U.S. Capitol building in Washington. Granny D, a ninety-year-old New Hampshire native who walked thirty-two hundred miles across the country to advocate campaign finance reform, recited a passage of the Declaration of Independence as the police placed her in handcuffs. She was charged with illegally demonstrating inside the Capitol building. She did not raise her voice or interfere with other visitors to the Capitol. "If it is a crime to read the Declaration of Independence in our great hall, then I am guilty," said Granny D at her court hearing.[3]

We must speak and debate openly and independently, without fear of rebuke from the government, if we are to maintain the exchange of ideas that supports intelligent voting, legislation, good government, and ultimately, freedom. And the point of this government is in turn to protect our right to those very debates that support such exchange of ideas; they are the essence of liberty and the project of the American democracy.

A society of people too terrified to wear colored socks or speak freely is a society that makes even sheep look bold. Can we keep the liberties and freedoms of the natural law if we are so quick to cower in the shadow of the government? Ours is a time for wolves.

> A society of people too terrified to wear colored socks or speak freely is a society that makes even sheep look bold.

5

VIETNAM—ALPHA, BRAVO, ELLSBERG

A team of oarsmen pulls a sleek shell down the Charles in early June, gliding by trees that seem to yearn for the river. The boat heads toward the MIT campus, past joggers in crimson jackets and old Volvos, where a congenial sort of man in a cardigan is leaving his office at the Center for International Studies. He hears the din of heavy Boston traffic and smiles as he wanders on foot to his apartment, to watch a lazy hour of television and perhaps doze off in the summer heat. He is a Harvard-trained economist, a researcher with intense and private reservations about the war in Vietnam. He is about to become the most wanted man in the United States. His name is Daniel Ellsberg.

Between 1964 and 1969, Professor Daniel Ellsberg contributed to a top secret study of the U.S. engagement with Vietnam, after serving there in a civilian capacity with the military. Secretary of Defense Robert McNamara had commissioned the report, which painted a picture of lies and deception surrounding the government's escalating role in the war. The forty-seven-volume, seven-thousand-page report showed that the United States had planned its involvement as far back as the Truman Administration, and that President

Lyndon B. Johnson had only pretended to consult advisors and the public before deciding to send troops. The report, which would later come to be called the "Pentagon Papers," also revealed that a victory in Vietnam was highly unlikely and probably impossible.

Professor Ellsberg's cynicism pervaded his contribution, and he realized that he could not stand by and watch the country send more young men to die for a cause that was likely to fail.

His first thought was to have a senator expose the document on the Senate floor, where the law protects such disclosures as long as the Congress is in session. Unfortunately, none of the senators that he approached wanted to be involved. Anyone who transmitted or disseminated the report to any senator would likely be charged with espionage or treason.

Desperate for a way to share the truth about the war with the rest of America, Ellsberg contacted Neil Sheehan at the *New York Times*. The *Times* agreed to run portions of the report, despite its top secret status. Suddenly, President Nixon and his lawyers turned their attention to Ellsberg's whereabouts. White House lawyers looked to stop publication with a court order, and Nixon sent his men to find Ellsberg and destroy his credibility with the public.

During a phone call with President Nixon, White House Chief of Staff Alexander Haig called the Ellsberg-orchestrated leak "a devastating security breach . . . of the greatest magnitude of anything [I've] ever seen."[1]

The government's lawyers managed to get an injunction preventing publication of the report. As the FBI scoured Boston and Cambridge for Daniel Ellsberg, Nixon's federal agents broke into Ellsburg's psychiatrist's office, looking for information they could use to discredit him. They found nothing. Professor Ellsberg went into hiding.

Meanwhile, back in the Oval Office, President Nixon raged to Secretary of State Henry Kissinger: "People have gotta be put to the torch for this sort of thing." Later, referring to Sheehan at the *Times*, Nixon called him "a bastard; he's been a bastard for years, on Vietnam."

And finally, of the impending legal battle, Nixon said, "It's . . . one of those fights where you don't . . . know how it's gonna affect you, but, boy, it's one we had to make; and, by God, it's one I enjoy . . . These bastards have gone too far this time."[2]

The Nixon Administration tried everything to crush the story before it became national news. Nixon fumbled to address the problem as the story grew, offering a solution: "I'd just start right at the top and fire some people. I mean whoever, whatever department it came out of, I'd fire the top guy."[3] Luckily for Nixon and the people named in the report, a federal appellate court ruled in favor of the government and prevented the *New York Times* from publishing excerpts for the fifteen-day period that preceded the Supreme Court decision on the matter.

The government argued that publishing the report on Vietnam would present a grave danger to the United States and aid the North Vietnamese. In a line of thought that is startlingly similar to the Bush Administration's reasoning today, Nixon mused in private, "I think what is very important in this is to find a way to get some strong language—like a massive breach of security—things of that sort, so that we can get something in the public mind—we're not just interested in making the technical case for the lawyers."[4] Jokingly, Nixon suggested that the government lawyers in the case "use some really high-flown adjectives."[5]

The Supreme Court rejected the government's arguments about national security. Although the Court might issue a gag order on the press in the future, it set down a firm requirement that the government must present substantial evidence showing the danger posed by publication of a report such as the Pentagon Papers. Since the primary danger in this case was embarrassment and public outrage, the Court permitted the *New York Times* to run the articles.

The legal outcome of the case, although it favors freedom of speech, was a mixed bag. The government managed to suppress a critical story of national interest for more than two weeks, while our soldiers were dying in Vietnam, and it paved the way for a "national security" check on the freedom of the press that threatens to expand wildly today.

The scandal surrounding the case, however, sent a clear message to the American public. The charges against Ellsberg were dropped, and White House Counsel Charles Colson was charged with obstruction of justice for the outrageous investigation of Ellsberg and the break-in at his psychiatrist's office. White House Chief of Staff H. R. Haldeman summed up the debacle, paraphrasing Donald Rumsfeld, who had discussed the issue earlier that morning: "Out of the gobbledygook comes a very clear thing: you can't trust the government; you can't believe what they say; and you can't rely on their judgment; and the—the implicit infallibility of presidents, which has been an accepted thing in America, is badly hurt by this, because it shows that people do things the president wants to do even though it's wrong, and the president can be wrong."[6]

We have not made much progress since the Pentagon Papers scandal. The *New York Times* still takes orders from the president and fails to publish articles that are critical of the administration. The paper suppressed the NSA wiretapping story, for example, which will be discussed later, for more than a year, and only covered it after numerous meetings with members of the Bush Administration. It seems that there are few wolves in the newspaper business these days.

CONGRESS CRACKS DOWN ON EXECUTIVE ABUSES

By the early 1970s, as the Watergate scandal unfolded in the head-lines, trust in the government evaporated as quickly as support for the war in Vietnam. When a series of troubling reports concerning a covert program known as COINTELPRO started appearing in the press, many members of Congress realized they had been too lax, too trusting, for too long.

BEWARE OF THE F.B.EYE!

COINTELPRO was an FBI program that implemented campaigns designed to infiltrate, neutralize, and undermine civil rights, antiwar, and other politically dissident groups, and authorized intelligence agencies to collect information on the personal and political activities of U.S. citizens through secret surveillance techniques, including warrantless wiretapping.

In 1975, within a year of President Nixon's resignation, the United States Senate Committee to Study Governmental Operations with Respect to Intelligence Activities (commonly known as the "Church Committee," for its chairman Senator Frank Church [D-ID]) convened to investigate the lawfulness of the CIA's and FBI's intelligence-gathering techniques. In its fourteen reports, the Church Committee documented more than *five hundred thousand intelligence files* containing information on American citizens and domestic organizations obtained through illegal wiretapping, criminal interception of private mail, and infiltration of groups by informants.

The report included evidence that each administration from Franklin D. Roosevelt to Richard Nixon had authorized wiretaps that provided the White House with purely political or personal information unrelated to national security. Some of the targets of the wiretaps included journalists, Supreme Court Justice William O. Douglas, senators, congressional staff members, law firms, lobbyists, and members of the general public who were critical of White House policy.[7] Additionally, the report revealed that from 1963 until his death in 1968, Martin Luther King Jr. was the target of an intensive campaign by the FBI to "neutralize" him as an effective civil rights leader. The FBI gathered information about Dr. King's activities through an extensive surveillance program in attempts to obtain information they could use to "completely discredit" him.[8]

The Church Committee reported that as far back as 1946, the FBI used wiretaps and bugs to collect intelligence against both American citizens and foreigners within the United States, without a warrant. So the FBI continually broke the laws it was supposed to enforce. Finding the pervasiveness of these techniques to be a clear violation of the Fourth Amendment protection against unreasonable search and seizure, the Church Committee advised implementation of strict controls on their use.

FISA: A SHORT OR LONG LEASH?

Appalled by the revelations of the Church Committee reports, Congress enacted the Foreign Intelligence Surveillance Act (FISA) as a means to rein in the executive branch and halt the use of illegal intelligence-gathering techniques. FISA, which contains specific guidelines limiting the use of domestic electronic surveillance, mandates that all government agencies obtain a warrant before conducting domestic surveillance. FISA also created the Foreign Intelligence Surveillance Court (FISC) to oversee requests for surveillance warrants against suspected foreign intelligence agents within the United States. FISA mandates that all government agencies obtain a warrant before conducting electronic surveillance. Warrants cannot be granted without a showing of probable cause to suspect criminality.

Of course, there is an exception. FISA allows the president to authorize warrantless surveillance if, after a review by the attorney general and FISC, there is probable cause to suspect the target is a foreign power or agent thereof.[9] "Foreign powers" are any foreign government or entity that is directed and controlled by a foreign government, a foreign-based political organization not substantially composed of United States persons, or a group engaged in international terrorism or activities in preparation therefor.[10] "Agents" of foreign powers are persons "other than a United States person" who act inside the United States as officers or members of a foreign power or engage in international terrorism activities.[11]

The statute specifically provides that warrantless surveillance is only allowed if there is no "substantial likelihood that the surveillance will acquire the contents of any communication to which a United States person is a party."[12] Under FISA, anyone who authorizes or engages in electronic surveillance that is not within the mandate of the statute is subject to both civil liability and up to five years' imprisonment for each unauthorized wiretap.[13]

Although FISA does aim to protect the rights of American citizens and, at least on paper, does so better than the lawless

COINTELPRO era, there are serious questions regarding its constitutionality. The Fourth Amendment specifically requires that before the government can search the property of any person, whether American or foreign, it must demonstrate to a judge (and the judge must agree) that there is probable cause of criminal activity on the part of the individual whose property the government wishes to search. It further states that only a judge can authorize a search warrant.

FISA is unconstitutional because it changed the probable cause of criminality requirement of the Fourth Amendment to probable cause to suspect association with a foreign power. The probable cause of criminality requirement is in the Constitution, which can only be changed by an amendment—which requires two-thirds of each house of Congress and three-quarters of all the state legislatures to concur—not by a simple vote in Congress.

But even FISA has some respect for constitutional liberty. Even though intelligence may be gathered through surveillance based on warrants issued on a lesser standard than the constitutionally mandated one of probable cause of criminal activity, FISA prohibits prosecutions based on evidence obtained from these warrants. Thus, if a FISA warrant, validly issued by FISC, reveals that one of the busboys in the Pentagon cafeteria is really a spy who beats his wife, he could not be prosecuted for either crime because the evidence of his crimes was obtained in violation of the Fourth Amendment. He could be deported, but not prosecuted.

> If a FISA warrant reveals that one of the busboys in the Pentagon cafeteria is really a spy who beats his wife, he could not be prosecuted for either crime because the evidence of his crimes was obtained in violation of the Fourth Amendment.

The Bush Administration argues that FISA is too slow to be effective in thwarting future terrorist attacks. But considering that Judge Royce Lamberth—who headed the FISA court for seven years—recently revealed that the FISA process was actually very flexible, and he himself approved warrant requests on the phone in the middle of the night, it is more likely that the Bush Administration wanted something more along the COINTELPRO lines.

> **"When the president does it, that means it's not illegal."**
>
> **—President Richard Nixon**

Six years after his resignation, President Richard Nixon famously told reporter David Frost, "When the president does it, that means it's not illegal." Thirty years and six presidents later, the corruption of the Nixon era is a memory we all hoped would recede into the dark shadows of history. But Nixon's legacy of political corruption, his lack of integrity, his lack of fidelity to the Constitution, and his rejection of natural rights have been resurrected.

AND THE NOOSE TIGHTENS . . .

With President George W. Bush at the helm, the executive branch has reached well beyond the limits of its authority and has launched a full-on assault on the natural rights and fundamental liberties protected from interference by our Constitution. Over the course of his two terms, nearly every constitutional right has suffered, except for those of gun owners. The First Amendment right to association no longer extends to groups that provide "material support" to terrorists. The Fifth Amendment guarantee of due process no longer applies to those the president decides are "enemy combatants." The privacy protected by the Fourth Amendment may now be invaded without warrants. The separation of powers that subjects each branch to the checks and balances of the others has been rejected entirely and replaced by an above the law mentality that allows the president to authorize torture of prisoners despite international treaties and federal laws prohibiting torture under all circumstances.[14]

The coming chapters will demonstrate that the Patriot Act and its secretive companions in the Bush arsenal in the war against freedom are a blatant and unapologetic rejection of our natural rights and fundamental liberties. All Americans should question how so many sheep can trust a government that has no respect for its Constitution or its people or their natural rights.

6

POST-SEPTEMBER 11TH: AN ORWELLIAN NEW WORLD?

CREATING A CULTURE OF FEAR

September 11th 2001 was a horrible day in human history. It marked the American psyche with a dark and jagged scar that will never fade or be forgotten. To the American people and lovers of freedom in the international community, it was a tragedy. To the Bush Administration, it was an opportunity.

In his prophetic and terrifying projection of the future, written in a novel entitled *1984*, George Orwell forecast a world in a perpetual state of war; a world where history is rewritten and existences are erased by the "Ministry of Truth"; where individual liberty is subordinate to party loyalty; a totalitarian society in which "Big Brother" is always watching.

The year 1984 came and went without the introduction of the newspeak dictionary or giant posters of a Stalinesque Big Brother figure gazing down omnisciently from every building and billboard; and everyone breathed a sigh of relief. But a mere generation later, there is an increasingly thin line between reality in the post-September 11th world and the fiction of *1984*.

In the aftermath of the attacks on the World Trade Center and the Pentagon, overcome by fear, grief, and anger, we became a passive society of sheep willing to allow the government to do whatever it deemed necessary to protect us from experiencing again the pain we felt on September 11th.

Instead of declaring a war against al-Qaeda, the admitted perpetrator of the September 11th attacks, the government came up with a new and ominous enemy. An enemy not bound by geography, ideology, or state authority. An enemy that could be lurking around every corner, in every subway station, aboard every airplane, mowing your lawn, pumping your gas, teaching your children. Within a few days of September 11th, the country was immersed in a "War on Terror." Grammar aside, the so-called "War on Terror" quickly became a war on Americans' privacy, freedom of movement, freedom of thought, individuality, and civil liberties.

Bomb squads were dispatched to full-time posts at the bridges and tunnels of major cities. Fatigue-clad officers with machine guns patrolled train terminals, subways, and airports. The headlines warned of anthrax and other biological-warfare threats and reported that the terror-alert meter remained in a constant elevated state. The country was shaken and afraid.

Soon, Washington tired of chasing the ghost of Osama bin Laden through the desert. With dollar signs in their eyes, they began pushing the "weapons of mass destruction" pitch for invading the new enemy in the war on terror: Saddam Hussein's Iraq. George W. Bush proclaimed, "Either you are with us, or you are with the terrorists."

> Soon, Washington tired of chasing the ghost of Osama bin Laden through the desert. With dollar signs in their eyes, they began pushing the "weapons of mass destruction" pitch . . .

With the population high on fear, and the media constrained by corporate and political pressures, the government began progressively dissolving our rights through a series of legislative and executive acts that concentrate power in the executive branch without congressional or judicial oversight.

Today, if the government decides you're a terrorist, without so much as being informed of the charges, you can be picked up by masked men, taken to a secret "black site" prison, and tortured until and unless you confess to being a terrorist; even if you're not. If they finally admit they picked up the wrong guy, you'll probably still be held so that you won't stir up bad publicity.

If you're a member of an activist organization or have ever blogged about how betrayed you feel by your government, or how you really wish they would end this futile war and bring your kid home from Iraq, your name might be on the terrorist watch list along with thousands of other innocent people. Your phone might be tapped, your computer might be monitored, and thousands of surveillance cameras may be focused on you as you trip over that crack in the sidewalk. Today, more than ever, Big Brother may literally be watching.

> **Today, more than ever, Big Brother may literally be watching.**

George W. Bush has repeatedly proclaimed that his Administration is committed to preserving and spreading democracy. But his policies paint a different domestic picture. The great dictators in history started small. First they create a terrifying threat. Under the fog of fear, they then begin chipping away at rights and liberties, in order to preserve "national security." They create prison camps that operate outside the law. They set up a domestic surveillance system and make sure the people know they are being watched. Then they begin harassing those who disagree with their policies or display insufficient political loyalty, such as intellectuals, politicians, and even government officials who fail to toe the line. Next they infiltrate and take control of the press. Finally, they assert "emergency authority" to suspend the rule of law.[1]

Sounds eerily familiar, doesn't it?

BUSH'S POWER GRAB:
THE USA PATRIOT ACT

In the weeks following September 11ᵗʰ while the country was still in a grieving state of shock and fear that another terror attack was imminent, a massive piece of legislation was introduced to Congress. The 342-page bill was strategically titled the "Uniting and Strengthening America by Providing Appropriate Tools Required to Intercept and Obstruct Terrorism Act of 2001" or, as it is popularly known, the USA PATRIOT Act, or simply the Patriot Act.

Under the assurances of Attorney General John Ashcroft that the tools within the Patriot Act were vital to protecting America from terrorists, the bill was passed in the Senate with little debate. In fact, only two senators read the complex and lengthy document: Paul Wellstone (D-MN) (now deceased) and Russ Feingold (D-WI). The bill, which was posted on the House intranet *fifteen minutes prior to the vote*, was not the same bill House members had seen in the days before the vote. The House leadership had replaced it. Thus, not a single House member read the bill in full before voting. But the bill passed with overwhelming majorities in both houses of Congress.

The text of the legislation itself proclaims its purpose is "to deter and punish terrorist acts in the United States and around the world, to enhance law enforcement investigatory tools, and *for other purposes.*" The contents of the Patriot Act amend at least fifteen separate federal laws including the Foreign Intelligence Surveillance Act of 1978 (FISA) and the Electronic Communication Privacy Act of 1986.[2]

Although you'd never know it from the catchy acronym, the result of the intentionally vague language within the Patriot Act is a brutal slaughter of essential freedoms in the name of national security. In granting the executive branch a laundry list of enhanced surveillance tools and virtual immunity from judicial review or Congressional oversight, the Act violates a number of federal laws and several constitutional rights, including those guaranteeing protection from federal interference by the First and Fourth Amendments.

Thanks to Section 213 of the Patriot Act, government officials can now search your home or office without notifying you until after the search has been completed, so long as there is "reasonable cause to believe that providing immediate notification . . . may have an adverse result."[3] How is the private citizen supposed to assert his constitutional right to challenge evidence against him if he doesn't know the government has taken it? What's worse, Section 213 is not limited to terrorism investigations but extends to all criminal investigations!

Section 215 manages to violate two Amendments to the Constitution *and* a federal law in one shot. Under FISA, the FBI has the authority to obtain personal records from common carriers (any organization that transports persons or goods, and offers its services to the general public), public accommodation facilities (which include hotels, restaurants, barber shops, zoos, gas stations, and funeral parlors, to name but a few),[4] physical storage facilities, and vehicle rental facilities. But FISA requires the FBI to obtain a warrant prior to requesting the records and mandates that there must first exist a showing of probable cause to believe that the person to whose records the FBI seek access is a "foreign power" or "agent."

But under Section 215, evidence showing such probable cause is *not* required. Section 215 abolishes even the limited protective boundaries provided for by FISA. The Patriot Act allows the FBI to obtain search warrants requiring the production of "*any tangible things* (including books, records, papers, documents and other items)." Claiming the desired records *may be related* to an ongoing terrorism investigation or intelligence activities is enough. Furthermore, where FISA limited record access to foreign powers and their agents, Section 215 allows the FBI to obtain records of U.S. citizens and lawful permanent residents.

The second part of Section 215 is an outrageous restraint on the right to free speech. The Patriot Act places a gag order on any person served with a self-written search warrant (commonly known as a National Security Letter, which will be discussed in detail in later chapters) for information, barring them from disclosing that the FBI has either sought or obtained information from them. If a town librarian tells a neighbor (or a spouse or a lawyer or the press or a federal judge in a public courtroom) that the government has taken her Internet browsing records, the innocent librarian can end up in a federal prison for five

> If a town librarian tells a neighbor that the government has taken her Internet browsing records, the innocent librarian can end up in a federal prison for five years because of her truthful speech.

years because of her truthful speech. What part of "Congress shall make no law abridging the . . . freedom of speech" does the Congress *not* understand?

With one sweepingly broad provision, the Patriot Act manages to deprive people of two constitutional rights with one unconstitutional search warrant. But Section 215 is only part of the attack on privacy and free speech. Section 216 grants the authority to intercept all forms of Internet activity. The government can install its new tracking system into an Internet Service Provider upon a government agent's certification that the information that he is seeking to obtain is "*relevant* to an ongoing criminal activity."

The tracking system, known as "Carnivore," collects *all communications*, not only the Web sites and routing addresses, but also e-mail messages, instant messages, keystrokes, Web page activity, and Internet telephone communications of everyone using the network.[5] Essentially, if you are working on a computer that is connected to a network that is being monitored by the feds without a search warrant, pursuant to the Patriot Act, the government will have a detailed record of everything you buy online, as well as your bank account and credit card numbers, address, phone number, etc.; every query you type into Google; every site you visit; every e-mail you send; and every comment you post on MySpace. Everything about your virtual life is being fed out of a machine somewhere in the recesses of the Pentagon, regardless of whether you are the target of a serious investigation or just some ordinary citizen. And all of this at the mere whim of a federal agent,

> Everything about your virtual life is being fed out of a machine somewhere in the recesses of the Pentagon, regardless of whether you are the target of a serious investigation or just some ordinary citizen.

without a search warrant issued by a judge upon probable cause of criminal activity, as the Constitution requires.

In order to get around that pesky "probable cause" requirement to tap phones and computer servers and conduct physical searches, Section 218 allows wiretaps and physical searches with simply a claim that a "significant purpose" of the wiretap is to gather foreign intelligence. They don't even have to prove it's the actual reason.

The Patriot Act also assaults the First Amendment in Section 805 by broadening the definition of "material support" to terrorist organizations to include "expert assistance or advice." Section 805 allows the government to prosecute anyone who provides "advice or assistance derived from scientific, technical, or other specialized knowledge"[6] to any group classified as a "foreign terrorist organization." This broad and pliable definition allows the government to prosecute lawyers, doctors, financial advisors, insurance agents, advocacy organizations, charity groups, teachers, dentists, auto mechanics, and a plethora of other professionals with "specialized knowledge" merely for doing their jobs, without any proof of complicity or intention to aid terrorists.

As Georgetown Law professor David Cole has remarked, Section 805 is "one of the most extreme of the Patriot Act's many terms, because it criminalizes pure speech without any requirement that the government show that speech has any connection to furthering terrorism."[7]

The material support laws, like the sedition laws, "are all designed to serve the same purpose: to give the government incredible discretion to go after people without proving they took part in any criminal or violent act," said Cole.[8] In other words, the government can now lawfully prosecute those whose *speech and ideas* it hates and fears.

Once the dust settled at Ground Zero, the public finally began paying some attention to the rollback of natural rights implemented through the Patriot Act. Public outcry over the NSA wiretapping and a secret White House torture memo forced the government to relent on some of the more extreme provisions in order to get Patriot Act II authorized in 2006. But protecting privacy was not the plan, and the Bush Administration was determined to achieve its goals. In the same sneaky and deceptive way it got the Patriot Act passed, the Administration slipped some of the most controversial provisions into other bills; bills that approved combat and intelligence funding.

GIVE HIM AN INCH . . .

The president held off signing this dubious new incarnation of power until December 13th 2003, a Saturday, and the very day that Saddam Hussein was captured.

While the media outlets were in a frenzy over the dramatic images of America's Second Most Wanted being dragged out of a rat hole somewhere in the desert, back in Washington, President Bush silently signed into law the Intelligence Authorization Act (IAA) for Fiscal Year 2004.

On the surface, IAA appropriates funds to intelligence activities. However, since it is difficult for members of Congress to oppose appropriation of funds for intelligence, IAAs make for a nice vehicle for the government to grab extra power without too much scrutiny.

Tucked into the IAA for Fiscal Year 2004 were several paragraphs that dramatically increased the government's authority to spy on all persons in America. The most damnable provision exponentially expands the scope of personal information that the FBI is able to obtain without a warrant.

Since the 1970s, the FBI has had the ability to gain access to records from financial institutions through use of self-written search warrants or National Security Letters already mentioned in terrorism and espionage investigations. But the IAA for 2004 has redefined the scope of the term *financial institutions* to include not only banks; credit card companies; and finance corporations; but also stock brokers; investment bankers; loan companies; currency exchange agencies; any issuer, redeemer, or cashier of travelers' checks, checks, and money orders; travel agencies; insurance companies; jewelers; pawn shops; Western Union and other businesses that transmit funds; casinos; real estate agents; car dealerships; phone companies; FedEx; and even the post office![9] If that is not bad enough, the directive also places a gag order, complete with stiff penalties (up to five years in prison), that prohibits businesses from disclosing to anyone, including their clients, that the FBI has requested records.

Congress didn't notice the significance of the provision until it was too late. I mean, let's face it; these bills are long and complex. Who has time to read every little provision? Funds for intelligence? Sounds worthwhile. Unfortunately, Congress, too, has been infected with passivity and all too often bows to the pressures of the executive branch.

What does this mean?

Picture yourself at home as you are about to open your mail on a Friday evening. Earlier that week, the FBI flagged you because you *knew* a suspicious person, and wrote itself a search warrant. It requested records from your bank, your cell phone provider, your package shipping company, and your lawyer's firm. As you slide a letter opener through another envelope bearing confidential and privileged communications between you and your attorney, you are the last among thousands of watchful eyes to learn what is taking place in your bitter divorce. The FBI knew that your son was getting an autographed baseball glove (to help calm him down)—and it knew when it would arrive before you did. The same agents saw how many calls it took to your mother-in-law for you to fight tearfully over primary custody of the kids. The law firm that bills out your attorney at $500 an hour was first in line to hand your file to the FBI, and it wouldn't tell you so if you sued it.

What does this mean?

Your mail? *Your* cell phone? *Your* lawyer? You are the LAST person any of these things belong to; your property and your life went out the door with the birth of the Intelligence Authorization Act for 2004, the death knell of your privacy.

. . . AND HE TAKES A MILE

The National Security and Homeland Security Presidential Directive 20/51; if you've never heard of this one, you're not alone. This directive, also known as the "National Continuity Policy," went widely unnoticed by the press because the White House didn't issue a press release after it was signed on May 9th 2007. Instead, they simply posted it on the White House Web site. Its existence probably isn't known to most of Congress, since presidential directives are not published in the *Federal Register* (the daily executive branch gazette, where all presidential proclama-

> *Your* mail? *Your* cell phone? *Your* lawyer? You are the LAST person any of these things belong to; your property and your life went out the door with the birth of the Intelligence Authorization Act for 2004, the death knell of your privacy.

tions and executive orders must be published as mandated by The Federal Register Act of 1935).[10] But those who are talking about it are terrified by its implications.

A *presidential directive* is a form of executive order that pertains to national security. It may be issued by the president without any congressional oversight. And a presidential directive is effective—unless a future president decides to overturn or edit it.

NSPD-51/HSPD-20 essentially concentrates power into the office of the president to coordinate any and all government and business activities in the event of a "catastrophic emergency." Sounds like a thinning out of the red tape that left thousands of people homeless while federal emergency trailers went unused in the aftermath of Hurricane Katrina, right? Just wait. The problem is that the pliable language in the directive creates the ability for a vast scope of executive authority without the checks and balances of the other branches of government. And in the hands of people as sinister and power hungry as those who rule and want to rule Washington, it is akin to a grant of dictatorial powers.

"Catastrophic emergency" is defined in the directive as "any incident, regardless of location, that results in extraordinary levels of mass casualties, damage, or disruption severely affecting the U.S. population, infrastructure, environment, economy, or government functions" including "localized acts of nature," "accidents," and "technological emergencies."[11] Under this vague definition, large-scale protests against the war in Iraq might be considered a "disruption severely affecting the U.S. population." A power grid failure that blacks out large parts of heavily populated areas could be a technological emergency. A bridge collapse on a major traffic artery of an American city, such as the collapse of the I-35W bridge in Minneapolis, could be a "disruption" of "infrastructure" affecting the populace. If the Israeli-Palestinian clash breaks into all-out war; if another tsunami hits Indonesia; if a volcano erupts in Japan; if Russia completes its retreat from democracy; if Vermont succeeds in seceding from the Union; if there's a tornado, a hurricane, or an oil spill; if a plague of fire ants invades Crawford, Texas . . . you get the picture: The president has given himself the primary and unchecked authority to decide what constitutes a catastrophe.

Under President Bush's directive, once the president does declare a state of emergency, he can take over *all government functions including the Congress and the federal courts and direct all private sector activities* to "ensure we will emerge from the emergency with an enduring constitutional government." The emergency state exists until the president decides it is over.

Where did he get the power to authorize this?

NSPD-51/HSPD-20 ignores the National Emergencies Act, a U.S. federal law passed in 1976 as a means to prevent a perpetual state of national emergency and formalize Congressional checks and balances on presidential emergency powers. President Bush's directive does not require the president to submit to Congress his determination that a national emergency exists and imposes no time limits on the duration of the emergency state.

THE WARNER ACT: A FORMULA FOR FASCISM

Couple all of this with the John Warner Defense Authorization Act of 2007 and you've got yourself the recipe for authoritarianism in a hurry.

The Warner Act subverts the long-standing Insurrection and Posse Comitatus Acts that imposed strict prohibitions on U.S. military involvement in domestic law enforcement.[12] The Warner Act authorizes the president to declare a public emergency and to station troops anywhere in America in order to "restore public order" in the event of a natural disaster, epidemic, or other serious public health emergency, terrorist attack or incident, or *other condition*.[13] In other words, in a presidentially declared state of emergency, the president also has the power to declare martial law.[14] Once the military has taken over our law enforcement and judicial systems, and the writ of habeas corpus is but a distant memory, authoritarianism won't be far off.

Since no one in Congress really seems to care about this megalomaniacal power grab, we'll just have to wait until the next scary animal-related flu, riot, or tropical storm to see how audacious the executive branch really is. And if (when?) that day comes, let's just hope that the American people will not be so distracted by fear that they unquestioningly believe the government is trying to

> Once the military has taken over our law enforcement and judicial systems, and the writ of habeas corpus is but a distant memory, authoritarianism won't be far off.

help them. Let's hope Americans across the country won't stand out on their porches, sheepishly waving tiny American flags and watching the tanks roll down their suburban streets, rounding up and arresting the protesting wolves, while the last burning embers of democracy are being smothered before their eyes.

OTHER SLIMY BEHAVIOR

If you're not convinced that the government is hell-bent on accumulating extreme amounts of power in the name of national security, the forthcoming chapters will finalize the exsanguinations of your skepticism. In other words, get ready for some sleepless nights.

There are the secret memos between the White House counsel and the president, urging him to adopt a new plan to skirt the Geneva Conventions, thus inoculating U.S. government officials from being tried for war crimes. There are the horrors that take place at the military prison down in Guantánamo Bay, Cuba, and the shady business of extraordinary rendition and secret CIA prisons overseas. There's the firing of eight U.S. attorneys who weren't being sufficiently pliable to achieve even more political clout; the enormous oil contracts granted to Halliburton, the vice president's company; the covert operations to destabilize the Iranian government; the restrictions on media coverage of the conflict in Iraq; the secret, warrantless domestic spying program and invocation of the "state secrets" privilege in order to avoid any challenges to the master plan.

> **Let's hope Americans across the country won't stand out on their porches, sheepishly waving tiny American flags and watching the tanks roll down their suburban streets.**

Oh, there's something to be afraid of, all right. In *1984*, George Orwell projected a bleak view of the future: "Always there will be the intoxication of power, constantly increasing and constantly growing subtler. Always, at every moment, there will be the thrill of victory, the sensation of trampling on an enemy who is helpless. If you want a picture of the future, imagine a boot stamping on a human face—forever."[15]

Yes, we should be afraid that the American way of life is in jeopardy. But contrary to what the government has convinced the sheep to believe, it's not the terrorists who are the most dangerous threat.

7

NATIONAL SECURITY: AN EXCUSE FOR ABUSE

A top the list of dark and disturbing tales from the Bush years (and there are many) are the dramatic steps taken by White House agents to maintain their illegal domestic eavesdropping program.

MORE HOLLYWOOD THAN HISTORY

On the night of March 10th 2004, Acting Attorney General James B. Comey was headed home from a late night at the Department of Justice when his cell phone rang. On the line was the chief of staff of Attorney General John Ashcroft, who relayed to Comey that Mrs. Ashcroft had received a call from the White House, possibly, as Comey relayed to the Senate Judiciary Committee, from the president himself, asking her to allow the president's then chief of staff, Andrew H. Card Jr., and his then White House counsel, Alberto Gonzales, to visit the attorney general in his hospital room. Mrs. Ashcroft had banned all visitors since her husband, who was recovering from gallbladder surgery, was extremely ill and disoriented. Comey knew immediately what Card and the future attorney general were up to.

After September 11th President Bush issued a secret order allowing the National Security Agency to spy on Americans' phone calls, e-mails, and other electronic communications without a warrant from the Foreign Intelligence Surveillance Court or from any other judge, as the Constitution requires. Because this program was illegal, violating FISA and the First and Fourth Amendments, President Bush later set up a process of oversight for it, so that he could claim legal justification should he or his agents get caught. The process mandated reauthorization by the attorney general every forty-five days. The primary requirement for reauthorization was certification by the attorney general personally that the program was lawful and constitutional.

In the early part of 2004, the Justice Department's Office of Legal Counsel underwent a change in leadership. Two of the Administration's most aggressive advocates of unrestrained executive authority, Jay Bybee, the head of the office, and his deputy, John Yoo, had left, and Jack Goldsmith had taken over. Under the supervision of Comey and Goldsmith, the Department of Justice engaged in an intensive evaluation of the program. After months of scrutiny, Comey, along with many leading Justice Department officials, determined that the program was not in compliance with the law. Comey discussed the matter with Ashcroft. Although he had repeatedly reauthorized the program in the past, according to Comey, this time the attorney general agreed that he could not sign off on the recertification. That same day, Aschroft fell ill and was taken to the hospital, where he remained in intensive care for over a week.

On March 9th 2004, two days prior to the deadline for reauthorization, Comey went to a meeting at the White House. In the presence of Gonzales, Card, Vice President Dick Cheney, and his lawyer, David S. Addington, Comey told the president that the Justice Department viewed the spying program as not in accord with the law or the Constitution, and that he, as acting attorney general, would not recertify it.

His opinion was not well received. Many top White House officials vehemently disagreed with the Justice Department's objections to the secretive program, including the vice president and the future attorney general, Alberto Gonzales.

So when Comey's phone rang in the dead of the night on March 10th, his stomach turned with the knowledge that the next day was the deadline for reauthorization of the program; and the White House was on a quest to take advantage of a very sick man.

Comey ordered his security detail to get him to George Washington University Hospital immediately. With emergency sirens blaring, they raced through the District of Columbia night. Comey, who stands six feet six inches in height, sprinted up the hospital stairs three steps at a time and into the darkened room where his formerly robust, domineering boss now lay drugged and incoherent from painkillers. By the bedside stood Mrs. Ashcroft, holding her husband's hand. Ashcroft was heavily medicated and barely conscious. Jack Goldsmith was also in the room.

In the moments before Card and Gonzales arrived, Comey frantically tried to rouse Ashcroft and brief him about what was happening. Comey feared Gonzales and Card would fraudulently coerce Ashcroft, who did not have the capacity to understand the situation, to sign the documents. Comey called FBI Director Robert S. Mueller III and asked him to instruct his agents not to allow Comey to be removed from the room for any reason. Seconds later, Gonzales and Card entered carrying an envelope.

Gonzales did all the talking. He displayed the envelope and told the groggy Ashcroft that he was there to get his approval. Then, in a stunning display of authority and conviction, Ashcroft lifted himself up and in very strong terms told Gonzales he would not be signing anything. "I am not the attorney general," Ashcroft said. "There is the attorney general," he continued, pointing at Comey. The two men did not acknowledge Comey. They turned and walked out of the room. According to Jack Goldsmith in his new book, *The Terror Presidency* (W. W. Norton, 2007), as they left, "Mrs. Ashcroft sticks out her tongue" to express her "strong disapproval."

Minutes later Card called the adjoining hospital room, which was being used as a makeshift "command center" during Ashcroft's stay. Comey took the call. Card angrily demanded that Comey come to the White House immediately. But after the conduct he had just witnessed, Comey refused to meet with Card without a witness present. Card replied, "What conduct? We were just there to wish him well." Imagine if they had wished him ill. Infuriated and shaken, Comey tracked down Solicitor General Ted Olson (Comey's next in command at the Department of Justice). At eleven o'clock that night, after meeting with Olson and other DoJ leadership, Comey proceeded to the White House, with Olson in tow.

Comey met with Card in the West Wing,[1] and explained that the DoJ was doing what the Constitution required. Feeling as though nothing had been resolved, Comey left the White House.

The next day, President George W. Bush reauthorized the program of government spying on Americans, in defiance of the advice of his own Department of Justice that warrantless domestic spying is unconstitutional and criminal.

The next day Comey prepared a letter of resignation along with as many as thirty other Justice Department officials including FBI director Mueller. "I couldn't stay, if the administration was going to engage in conduct that the Department of Justice had said has no legal basis. I just simply couldn't stay," Comey told the Senate Judiciary Committee three years later. The program was so blatantly illegal that the top legal minds in the Department of Justice, lawyers appointed by the president, would rather resign than associate themselves with it.

Fearing that Ashcroft would be left behind to clean up the mess and shoulder the blame, his chief of staff asked Comey to stay through the weekend until Ashcroft was well enough to understand fully what was going on. Comey agreed.

The next day Comey reported to the Oval Office with FBI Director Mueller to brief the president on what was going on in the DoJ's counterterrorism work. As he was leaving, the president asked to speak to him in private.

> "I couldn't stay, if the administration was going to engage in conduct that the Department of Justice had said has no legal basis. I just simply couldn't stay."
> —Acting Attorney General James B. Comey, 2004

As usual, the content of this one-on-one exchange is classified, as is the content of the subsequent discussion President Bush had with Director Mueller. Perhaps it was because Bush knew that no amount of September 11th references, scare tactics, or sweet-talking charm would allow him to avoid impeachment if it was leaked to the media that he had knowingly authorized something his own Department of Justice had told him was illegal. But at the end of these private talks, without the influence of Andrew Card or Alberto Gonzales, or the acquiescence of John Ashcroft, the president directed Jim Comey and the Department of Justice to do whatever they needed to do to put the program on a sound legal footing.

Comey would not discuss the revisions that were made or the legal rationale for the revised program, but he did eventually authorize it.

This story sounds as if it were written for the next Hollywood political thriller, starring Matt Damon as the champion of constitutional rights, ready to quit before relenting on what he sees as an unethical violation of the law, taking on White House powermongers (played by Ben Affleck as the president, Joe Pesci as the manipulative White House counsel, and Jack Nicholson as the hot-tempered vice president who's getting his way). But it was very real. And it was a perfect example of the intellectual corruption and above-the-law attitude of the Bush Administration.

Needless to say, this story caused quite a stir at the Senate Judiciary hearing at which Comey testified. "When we have a situation where the laws of this country . . . are not respected because somebody thinks there's a higher goal, we run askew of the very purpose of what democracy and rule of law are about," said a visibly outraged Senator Charles E. Schumer (D-NY).[2] Under the Bush Administration, the White House handles Justice Department business, Schumer told the *Washington Post*, and "the vice president's fingerprints are all over the effort to strong-arm approval of the NSA domestic spying program."[3]

> "... the vice president's fingerprints are all over the effort to strong-arm approval of the NSA domestic spying program."
> —Senator Charles E. Schumer (D-NY)

Still, after this loathsome conduct was revealed in May 2007, the ethically challenged attorney general remained in office for another three months with full support of the president. When the Senate Judiciary Committee questioned Gonzales and he testified, senators claimed he systematically lied when he stated that he was not aware of any disagreement over the lawfulness of the program. Bush played the "state secrets" card and declined to comment on the incident. Cheney's involvement barely made the front page.

Both Congress and the media failed to question the president's role or whether he broke the law by authorizing the spying program without the approval of the attorney general. The media talked about it for a minute and then got distracted by "Paris Hilton Goes to Jail." But the fact remains: The president authorized a domestic surveillance program that the top legal advisors at the Department of Justice told him was illegal and unconstitutional. Where is the outrage?

George W. Bush insists that eavesdropping on the telephone calls and reading the e-mails of American citizens are crucial to national security and the prevention of future terrorist attacks. And maybe, in some extreme cases, where an American citizen has proven ties to terrorist organizations and there is probable cause for a court to issue a warrant for the wiretap, it is. That's why Congress enacted FISA, which itself is constitutionally questionable, but has at least established some guidelines and judicial oversight of the use of wiretapping and electronic surveillance.

Former chief of the Foreign Intelligence Surveillance Court (FISC) Judge Royce C. Lamberth said that the FISC approved 99 percent of applications, and he had personally approved warrants over the phone while in his car, from his home at 3 a.m., and on Saturdays. In fact, while Judge Lamberth was stuck in traffic after a hijacked jet slammed into the Pentagon on September 11th, he approved FISA warrants from his cell phone.[4] But the FISA process of filing an application in support of the request was too cumbersome a procedure for the president. Instead, the Bush Administration decided to claim the power to order warrantless spying without any evidence or process of review.

> **While Judge Lamberth was stuck in traffic after a hijacked jet slammed into the Pentagon on September 11th, he approved FISA warrants from his cell phone.**

What's worse is that the government is not just watching suspected terrorists. Although the president calls it the "terrorist surveillance program," conveniently, the government does not follow one strict definition of "terrorist." The guidelines defining who can be monitored are basically nonexistent. As a result, innocent, law-abiding citizens of this country are being secretly monitored, robbed of their fundamental civil liberties guaranteed in the Constitution.

The government is most likely listening to and recording the private conversations of lawyers and their clients, journalists and their sources, priests and their penitents, doctors and their patients, federal judges and their clerks, corporate chieftains and their personal assistants, scholars, antiwar organizations, veterans, former FBI agents, members of Congress, and probably even suspected weak links in the DoJ itself. It has reached a point where anyone critical of the Bush Administration is a potential threat to national security and, therefore, a wiretapping target.

But all of this has been remedied by the revisions authored by Jim Comey, right?

Wrong.

Although Comey comes out looking like Jimmy Stewart, the modified version of the clandestine eavesdropping program still violates the Fourth Amendment privacy protections and the First Amendment guarantee that you don't have to censor who you talk to, what you say, or the contents of your e-mails for fear that your government might secretly be listening.

If this is the version Comey approved, it is frightening to consider what must have been in the original. Telescreens monitored by the NSA? "Thought Police"[5] in every home in America? Computers programmed to act as government spies? Corporate informants of Americans who are not acting patriotic enough? These *1984* references are unsettlingly akin to the potential of the NSA domestic surveillance program.

STANDING UP FOR OUR RIGHTS

It sounds scary, but all hope is not lost. In December 2005, a *New York Times* report exposed that President Bush had secretly authorized the NSA to spy on Americans without warrants or even probable cause to believe the target was a terrorist, spy, or otherwise posed a threat to national security.[6] Immediately following the exposé, outraged legal scholars led the charge in challenging the executive branch's use of the cloak of "national security" to claim authority to ignore the Constitution and violate the inherent rights of the American people.

In January 2006, the scholars filed suit on behalf of a group of attorneys, journalists, scholars, and nonprofit organizations challenging the lawfulness of the NSA electronic surveillance program. The program was authorized by secret order of the president in 2002, without Congressional approval. It allows the NSA to monitor telephone and e-mail communications of people inside the United States, including American citizens, with persons abroad, without a court-approved warrant or any showing of probable cause. The program under scrutiny in the suit was the Comey-modified version that followed the Ashcroft hospital debacle.

In a landmark ruling, United States District Court Judge Anna Diggs Taylor, sitting in Detroit, held that the program violates the First and Fourth Amendments to the Constitution, the separation of powers doctrine, and the Foreign Intelligence Surveillance Act (FISA).

Judge Taylor's decision is merely an adherence to legal precedent across the United States that demands a court-ordered warrant for electronic surveillance to be lawful, even in cases involving domestic security and FISA. "Although many cases hold that the President's power to obtain foreign intelligence is vast, none suggest that he is immune from Constitutional requirements," wrote Judge Taylor.[7] She explained: "It was never the intent of the Framers to give the President such unfettered control, particularly where his actions blatantly disregard the parameters clearly enumerated in the Bill of Rights. The three separate branches of government were developed as a check and balance for one another. It is within the court's duty to ensure that power is never 'condense[d] . . . into a single branch of government.'"[8]

Judge Taylor denied the government's motion to dismiss the lawsuit on the basis of the state secrets doctrine (which will be further discussed later in this book), and ordered the president to shut down the NSA spying program.

"There are no hereditary kings in America and no [federal] powers not created by the Constitution," Judge Taylor declared.[9]

The government appealed Judge Taylor's determination that the challenge to the program could proceed without exposure of classified information. Before the Sixth Circuit Court of Appeals, the

Department of Justice once again invoked the state secrets privilege, claiming the program is immune from judicial review due to its "highly classified" nature. "Litigating even the standing of plaintiffs to maintain this action, let alone the legality of the surveillance program, would reveal extraordinarily sensitive intelligence information that, if disclosed, would cause the nation grievous injury."[10]

In July 2007, the Sixth Circuit dismissed the case. Without consideration of the constitutional issues, the court found the challenge could not proceed because the plaintiffs were unable to prove they were actually the victims of the NSA wiretaps. The records necessary to prove this are classified under the state secrets doctrine. Because no plaintiffs will ever have access to the documents necessary to prove they were the victims of warrantless surveillance, this ruling effectively insulates the wiretapping program from future judicial scrutiny.

The majority focused entirely on the plaintiffs' standing to sue. They declined to address any of the serious constitutional issues presented by the case or offer an opinion as to the lawfulness of the warrantless surveillance program. However, in a dissenting opinion, Judge Ronald Lee Gilman, the only judge to discuss the merits of the challenge, unequivocally agreed with Judge Taylor's opinion that the surveillance program violates at least FISA and the Separation of Powers Clause of the Constitution.

Facing certain appeal to the Supreme Court and fearing that the plaintiffs were still committed to protecting the Constitution and natural rights, the Administration, through the ever-loyal Attorney General Gonzales, claimed it had resumed submitting requests for wiretapping warrants to the FISA court, thus mooting the case. Considering that Gonzales is potentially facing perjury charges for lying about the very same program, that seems highly unlikely. But the

statement is an unarticulated recognition that the warrantless surveillance program violates the law and will not survive the scrutiny of the
highest court in the land. The executive branch is afraid the Supreme
Court will rein in its lawless behavior.

On July 4th 2001, President Bush addressed the people of
Philadelphia. He spoke of America as a country where freedom is
the birthright of every individual, and equality is granted by the
design of our Creator. "Natural rights, not for the few, not even for
a fortunate many, but for all people in all places, in all times,"[11] the
president proclaimed. Six years later, it appears he forgot to mention
that natural rights are subject to a laundry list of terms and conditions and may be withdrawn at the discretion of the Chief Executive.

8

NO WARRANT?
NO PROBLEM

The sheep among us want to believe that our civil liberties are not really in danger, that the government is protecting us from terrorism, and that the wolves are just being paranoid.

Setting aside the volumes of other evidence for the moment, when the Inspector General of the Department of Justice concludes that too many liberties are being sacrificed for security, it seems reasonable to be a bit concerned. But despite hard evidence that our government has systematically abused its power and violated our constitutional rights through the FBI's use of self-written search warrants, the sheep among us continue to ignore the reality that freedom is in serious jeopardy.

The government, in its never-ending campaign to sanitize its criminal undertakings, calls the self-written search warrants "National Security Letters." These are among the most dynamic intelligence-gathering tools of the post-September 11th era. The warrant allows the government to demand that telephone companies, banks, credit bureaus, Internet service providers, storage facilities, pawn shops, real estate brokers, physicians, lawyers, and virtually any other business that maintains personal records (thanks to IAA04's revision of the "financial institutions" definition as discussed in Chapter 6) turn over those personal records of their customers without a judge-approved warrant, probable cause, or any judicial oversight.[1]

National Security Letters (NSLs) have been used since the late 1970s, but prior to the Patriot Act, their use was limited to obtaining financial and communications records of persons who the FBI had probable cause to believe were agents of foreign powers involved in terrorism and espionage investigations. NSLs had to be approved by FBI headquarters, and compliance with the request was voluntary.[2] Further, the information gathered could not be used as evidence in a criminal case, because the Constitution only permits the government to use evidence obtained from warrants that judges, not FBI agents, have issued.

But along with many other liberty-crushing provisions, the Patriot Act gave life to a Frankensteinian incarnation of the NSL. The government may now use NSLs to seize unconstitutionally the private records of U.S. citizens and legal residents who are not suspected of any criminal conduct, so long as "the information sought is *relevant* to an authorized investigation to protect against international terrorism or clandestine intelligence activities."[3] The language sets absolutely no limit on the type or number of records subject to the NSLs, leaving open the potential for an NSL to demand entire phone company or financial databases. One single NSL has the potential to release the records and destroy the constitutionally guaranteed privacy of millions of Americans.

Instead of submitting evidence and allowing a judge to decide what is relevant, NSLs may now be authorized by anyone "in a position not lower than Deputy Assistant Director at Bureau headquarters or a Special Agent in Charge in a Bureau field office."[4] The FBI has fifty-six field offices across the United States and Puerto Rico, which means at least fifty-six "Special Agents in Charge" are authorized to issue NSLs (assuming that "in charge" is intended to mean "of the office itself" and not the specific investigation, which seems unlikely). At FBI headquarters there are at least twenty-five people holding positions with the title Deputy Assistant Director or above.[5]

In addition, section 505 of the Patriot Act extends the once-exclusive FBI privilege to other federal agencies, such as the CIA and the Department of Defense.[6] Considering that the legal scope of the term *relevant* is extremely broad[7] and left entirely to the discretion of no fewer than eighty-one people, the door is left wide open for abuse.

And abuse it they have.

In 2007, despite the objections of the White House, the Department of Justice conducted a congressionally mandated audit of the FBI's use of NSLs. The results revealed widespread misuse of this highly invasive authority.

The audit revealed more than a thousand violations within a 10 percent sample of investigations involving National Security Letters. Many of the violations involved failures to obtain proper authorization, as well as the collection of information to which the FBI was not entitled. Fifty-three percent of NSL requests targeted U.S. citizens.[8]

In addition to the improper and often illegal use of the letters against Americans, few of whom are suspects in any terrorism, intelligence, or criminal matter, the FBI officially, as an entity, lied to Congress about the number of NSLs that were issued. The National Security Letter database (which is reported to Congress annually) recorded 143,074 NSLs issued between 2003 and 2005. However, the audit revealed an average of 22 percent more NSLs in the case files than were recorded.

Unfortunately, the government's contempt for fundamental civil liberties isn't limited to illegal collection of information on millions of innocent Americans who have no way of knowing whether their government has a file on them in its ever-expanding database.

DRAFTED INTO SECRET SERVICE

Three years ago, "John Doe," the president of a small Internet consulting business, was drafted into service as an informant for the FBI. John received a National Security Letter requesting the records on one of his clients. The letter contained a gag order that prohibited John from telling anyone, including the client, that the FBI had requested the information, or from revealing his involvement in the case in any way. The letter did not *ask* for his cooperation; it *demanded* compliance under threat of criminal prosecution.

But John is not a sheep. He dodged the draft, and instead of turning over the information, John filed a lawsuit challenging the constitutionality of the NSL power.[9]

While Congress was debating the reauthorization of the Patriot Act in 2005, John was unable to voice his concerns to his representatives, discuss his experiences in a public forum, or advocate changes in the law. The NSL gag order deprived John of his constitutional right to free speech and to petition the government for redress of grievances.

A GAGGLE OF GAG ORDERS

When the FBI demanded access to records showing the Internet activity of patrons of a Connecticut library, a group of intrepid librarians refused to be herded into compliance.[10]

Outraged over the government's secret attempt to investigate what the public is informing itself about, but silenced under the NSL's gag order, the librarians recruited freedom-loving lawyers to act on their behalf. They filed a suit challenging the constitutionality of the NSL gag order and charged the government with sweeping violations of their First Amendment rights.[11]

In *Doe v. Ashcroft* and *Doe v. Gonzales*, the federal district courts in New York City and Bridgeport, Connecticut, stood up for the constitutional rights of John Doe and the librarians. Both courts declared that the NSLs' permanent gag orders violate the First Amendment. The courts enjoined the government from issuing NSLs and from enforcing the nondisclosure provision in these or any other cases.

The government appealed, and the Second Circuit Court of Appeals combined the cases. Because the USA Patriot Improvement and Reauthorization Act had been passed—amending some language in Section 505 that was relevant to the original decision—the New York case was remanded back to the district court for a new trial.

Even though the FBI has decided it no longer needs the records it originally requested, the real recipient of the NSL remains under a gag order that prevents him from revealing his experience. While preparing for the new trial, he has been forced to lie to colleagues, friends, and family. "When I meet with my attorneys, I cannot tell my girlfriend where I am going or where I have been. I hide any papers related to the case in a place where she will not look."[12]

The Connecticut case was dismissed because, nearly a year after the FBI had discredited the potential terrorism threat that had led to the request, the government lifted the gag order on the librarians—eliminating their standing to sue.

"The fact that I can speak now is a little like being permitted to call the fire department only after a building has burned to the ground," said George Christian, one of the four librarians at the center of the dispute with the FBI, after the gag order was finally lifted.

Without hearing from their constituents who were personally violated by the NSLs, Congress reauthorized the gag-order provision with minor amendments. The revisions give the illusion that the gag order can be appealed. In actuality, those who receive NSLs are bound by the gag order for one year before they can apply for an appeal. Even then, the gag will be upheld if the FBI says it is needed for national security. The FBI continues to have *carte blanche* authority to issue NSLs, as there is still no judicial oversight requirement, in direct contradiction to the Constitution.

After the revelations of the Department of Justice report, the FBI implemented new guidelines for internal controls with regard to the issuing process of NSLs. But the authority has been abused in the past. Do we really believe they will adhere to the guidelines the next time our backs are turned?

The government says, "Trust us." They say that the NSL and its gag order are necessary tools to protect you from terrorism. But without any guidelines or limits, do we really trust that the use of NSLs is limited to terror investigations?

The drafters of the Constitution explicitly intended to protect our natural rights from the threat of unlimited government. But the National Security Letter is a blank check for unrestricted access to our private lives.

What if the FBI could use NSLs to collect records on journalists, lawyers, politicians, activists, or anyone who expresses politically unpopular views? The reckless misuse by the FBI and its blanket of secrecy that keeps NSL opponents gagged leaves open the potential for a new era of criminal justice: An era in which privacy is only possible if you never buy, say, or do anything that will leave a physical record that may later be used to incriminate you; an era in which the Constitution is meaningless and the government can do to anyone whatever it wants, like the regimes of Hitler, Stalin, and Mao Tse-tung.

Just to be prepared for the possibility that someday you might be suspected of some miscellaneous crime that the government doesn't really have any evidence you committed, you should go ahead and cancel your subscription to *Guns & Ammo*. Stock up on quarters for all the calls you'll be making from pay phones. Close your bank accounts, and start stuffing your mattress with cash. Send one last good-bye e-mail to all your friends, and then sell your laptop on Craigslist. Hell, just avoid suspicion altogether, and move to a log cabin somewhere deep in the woods, and become one with nature.

If our fear of terror makes us give up the rights that make us free, then the terrorists have won.

> **You should go ahead and cancel your subscription to *Guns & Ammo*. Stock up on quarters for all the calls you'll be making from pay phones. Close your bank accounts, and start stuffing your mattress with cash. Send one last good-bye e-mail to all your friends, and then sell your laptop on Craigslist.**

9

STATE SECRETS:
EXPLOITING
THE PRIVILEGE

In 1953, the Supreme Court handed the government a conces-
sion in a small—at the time seemingly unimportant—case.
Three widows of men who died in a plane crash sued over the
government-operated flight, in an attempt to learn what had happened to their husbands. The husbands, employees of RCA and
the Franklin Institute, were researchers hired by the federal government to test a new electronics system aboard a military aircraft.
Unfortunately for the widows, this plane happened to be a B-29
Super Fortress, the very same model used to drop the atomic bombs
in Japan.

The Soviets had reverse-engineered the B-29 in the form of
their Tupolev Tu-4 plane, and it had many of the same serious
design defects. When the B-29 plane carrying Patricia Reynolds's
husband crashed during the test flight over Waycross, Georgia,
government officials were quick to claim that disclosure of the
flight details might shed light on the defects of the B-29 bomber,
and somehow inadvertently aid the Soviets. In other words, government lawyers argued that the reports on the crash contained

alleged "state secrets," which could not be released in court without endangering national security.

Like other special evidentiary privileges recognized by courts of law, the privilege protecting state secrets requires that the judge determine whether or not the privilege should apply and, if it does, how the case should proceed without revealing the sensitive material. Often a case will not need to be thrown out; rather, the court will work around the privileged evidence to resolve the plaintiff's claims.

This is precisely what the Supreme Court did in the Reynolds case. The widows, Phyllis Brauner, Elizabeth Palya, and Patricia Reynolds, accepted a settlement with the government on the basis of the incomplete evidence available to the court. Each of the widows received about $40,000, which is worth roughly $300,000 today. But fifty years later, Palya's daughter learned that the settlement was the result of a scandal: $40,000 was the price the government was willing to pay to bury three innocent victims and one embarrassing truth.

Judith Loether, Elizabeth Palya's daughter, found the flight report on the Internet in 2003. A quick read through the document showed that state secrets had nothing to do with the government's defense in the Reynolds case. Actually, the B-29 was simply a danger-

> $40,000 was the price the government was willing to pay to bury three innocent victims and one embarrassing truth.

ously designed plane, riddled with defects, and the pilot, though experienced, failed to resolve a malfunction during the flight. The report suggests that he nervously hit the wrong switch after one of the engines cut out. With a fire building over the engine, he was unable to keep the plane aloft. The government invoked the state secrets defense to avoid the embarrassing truth and costly liability for negligence in failing to discontinue use of the faulty aircraft. And the court allowed it, unwittingly giving birth to what has become a heavyweight scandal in the present administration's arsenal.

The Supreme Court rejected Loether's petition to have the case reheard, and a federal court in Pennsylvania (where the case originated) also refused to hear her claim. The case is settled, and the federal government abused and defrauded three innocent widows. The state secrets defense has become law, and the current administration is taking full advantage of it.

When an affidavit from a government official, without evidence or detail, is enough to support a claim for the legal privilege of state secrets, the military, and the government that controls it, is no longer accountable to the people or the courts.

What's worse is that the government has gone beyond using the privilege to suppress evidence and, as it did in the B-29 case, has actually manipulated the courts into an excuse for closing cases altogether. In step with the beat of the Bush Administration's war song, the state secrets privilege brings the cry of military necessity to the civilian courts, where the once-sacred rule of law is now drowning in a deluge of extraconstitutional executive power.

Now the testing ground for the state secrets doctrine extends far beyond remote sites and ten-man plane flights. Now this once-unremarkable legal maneuver has become the inscrutable shield for covert operations across the United States and around the world.

As National Security Agency offices are secretly cropping up within AT&T's buildings, and the same cables that carry our phone calls and e-mails diverge to make stops in small, unmarked rooms in NSA strongholds within our telecom companies, it seems only a matter of time before all of us are forced to acknowledge the very real war on privacy and personal security that we are currently losing to our own government. And the courts have been silent partners to the executive zeitgeist, until one court remembered the Constitution in a recent case.

AT&T: YOUR WORLD
DELIVERED . . . TO WHOM?

In 2006, California residents Tash Hepting and two other AT&T subscribers, aware of AT&T's unseemly sheepish compliance with the federal government's illegal demands to facilitate a warrantless surveillance program, brought a suit against the company, claiming damages for the millions of people affected by the program daily. Hepting also asked the court to halt the program, which compiles a record of all telephone calls and Internet usage by subscribers for the past several years in a massive database called "Daytona." Each business day, AT&T transmits and records a total amount of data that is more than two hundred times the size of the entire Library of Congress, the world's largest library. If the library's shelf space were that large, it would stretch about halfway to the moon!

> Each business day, AT&T transmits and records a total amount of data that is more than two hundred times the size of the entire Library of Congress, the world's largest library.

An AT&T employee who testified for Hepting, Mark Klein, told the court that the sheer volume of data being collected makes it difficult to believe that Daytona only targets suspects in terrorist investigations. In fact, the odds are that many if not all of our calls and e-mails are recorded, traced, or monitored on networks such as AT&T's.

It is a violation of our First Amendment right to freedom of speech to have to conduct every conversation as though government agents were listening. Imagine having the federal government on a conference call as you tell your spouse about plans for dinner or speak to your children. What about casual conversations with friends? Or calls with your lawyer, accountant, physician, priest, rabbi, or imam?

Until the recent lawsuits against AT&T and similar companies are resolved, there isn't much that we can do about the NSA's prying eyes and probing ears. Programs like Zfone allow computer users to make protected, encrypted phone calls over the Internet, but they are extremely complex and hardly user-friendly. Prepaid cellular phones are an option for the concerned, or for those in the "waste management" industry.

Understandably, the plaintiffs in the Hepting lawsuit tried to include the millions of other affected subscribers in the case to add weight to their claims and strengthen their attack against the NSA surveillance program.

AT&T also added a party to its side. When Hepting brought the suit and dragged the NSA program into the public eye, the government was quick to intervene and join AT&T as a defendant. Concerned about the spotlight on its illegal and covert spying program, the government invoked its trusty state secrets defense in an effort to quash the case before it began.

In a surprising turn of events, judicial responsibility and candor overcame the government's privilege. The court allowed Hepting to bring evidence against AT&T. Although it noted that state secrets might play a role in preventing some evidence from being procured, the court rebuffed the use of the state secrets defense as a way to prevent cases from being tried at all.

Judge Vaughn Walker, a federal district judge in San Francisco, California, appointed by President Ronald Reagan, wrote in the Hepting decision: "The court . . . takes seriously its constitutional duty to adjudicate the disputes that come before it . . . to defer to a blanket assertion of secrecy here would be to abdicate that duty."[1] Quoting the highly publicized U.S. Supreme Court decision in *Hamdi v. Rumsfeld,* Judge Walker warned of the burgeoning imperative of the executive branch: "Whatever power the United States Constitution envisions for the Executive in its exchanges with other nations or with enemy organizations in times of conflict, it most assuredly envisions a role for all three branches when individual liberties are at stake."

Courts have not always been so conscious of the importance of standing up to the executive branch when it asserts the state secrets privilege. In one study, a professor at the University of Texas found that the government used its privilege only four times between 1953 and 1977, but that between 1977 and 2001, it was used more than fifty times; and it never failed, until it met Judge Walker.[2] With government approval ratings dipping below 30 percent, the executive branch has a greater incentive than perhaps ever before to cover up scandals and questionably legal policies and programs with the state secrets doctrine.

YE ARE NOT YOUR OWN . . .

The government has even manipulated the doctrine to block an inventor's patent, in a bizarre case involving Lucent Technologies, a telecommunications company that spun off from AT&T.

Philip French, the inventor of the Crater Coupler, a device used to connect pipes seamlessly, negotiated a deal with Lucent to apply the technology to underwater fiber-optic pipelines for potential government and military use. The design, which French derived from the interlocking halves of a tennis ball, was worth at least half a million dollars in licensing fees to French's partners. But after a year of working with Lucent, the company notified French and his partners that it would not pay them a dime. It later offered French $100,000, which was several hundred thousand dollars below his expectations and possibly millions below the device's value. Lucent's angle? A federal agency was willing to step in and play the state secrets card on Lucent's behalf.

> The navy's maneuvers may or may not have protected a military endeavor, but they undeniably neglected French's constitutional right to control his own patented invention.

Secretary of the Navy Richard Danzig stated that French's defense of his patent rights, if conducted in court, "could be expected to cause extremely grave damage to national security." The federal district judge in the case, Richard Webber, examined the government's documents privately to determine whether or not the state secrets privilege applied. He reviewed some twenty-six thousand documents and determined that, as a whole, they constituted a state secret. This effectively blocked all of the patent claims against Lucent. A federal appellate court upheld Judge Webber's decision.

French and his colleagues received little for their efforts or their innovation, except for publicity and sympathy from the media. The navy's maneuvers may or may not have protected a military endeavor, but they undeniably neglected French's constitutional right to control his own patented invention. In light of the disclosure of the classified material in the Reynolds case, French is no doubt uncertain as to whether his lost retirement funds were taken from him to hide a mere embarrassment or another government scandal.

THE CONSTITUTION PROJECT

A group of lawyers and legal scholars has spoken out on the judiciary's right to oversee executive action, despite the growth of the state secrets doctrine. The Constitution Project, headed by members of law firms, professors, and congressmen, held a panel discussion in May 2007 and formally issued an evaluation of the doctrine.

The panel urged Congress to pass a law providing courts with specific guidelines for handling cases where the government claims its privilege. The statement, titled "Reforming the State Secrets Privilege," argues that, in particular, judges should demand the ability to review in private documents alleged to contain purported secrets before accepting a government agency's assertion of the defense. If possible, the plaintiff should be allowed to proceed, even in a case where the state secrets doctrine applies. All its proposals fell on deaf ears. The large number of lawyers signing the Constitution Project statement indicates the severity of the problem. It may take the coordinated effort of the legislative and judicial branches to combat the abuse of this privilege.

MORE STEPS TOWARD SUBJUGATION

As long as the government continues to raise the state secrets privilege successfully, it will discover new uses for the doctrine and new ways to intervene in the administration of justice. In coordination with the extraordinary rendition program that the CIA runs to torture terrorist suspects outside of the United States, the privilege provides a cloak for disgraceful violations of human rights. The first of these trials, involving an Egyptian cleric, Hassan Mustafa Osama Nasr, has finally begun after Nasr was kidnapped by CIA agents in Milan four years ago. But depending on the Italian Constitutional Court's analysis of Italy's state secrets privilege, the court may throw out Nasr's case and let him try his claims of torture in the international media.

The French have also caught on to the state secrets craze, clamping down on a surprising source of breaches of security: The harmless BlackBerry. According to Alain Juillet, the head of French Economic Intelligence, the use of BlackBerrys by French officials for important communications is dangerous because "the risks of interception are real." He claims that France is in the middle of an "economic war" with the United States, and that sensitive e-mails, which must travel through BlackBerry computer servers in Britain and the United States, are part of this war. With the NSA spying illegally on American citizens, maybe Juillet has a point.

> The French have also caught on to the state secrets craze, clamping down on a surprising source of breaches of security: The harmless BlackBerry.

And forget about freedom of speech in China—what *isn't* a state secret there? The government has posted an official set of topics that may not be discussed in the media, because of their relevance to state secrets. What qualifies as a state secret in China? Information about natural disasters. Statistics about those killed or wounded in war. Facts about public health crises. Plans for national land use. Even weather reports and "environmental quality" statements are considered state secrets. This means that the government could punish a Chinese newspaper, television station, or Web site for publishing information about bird flu!

Will courts across the world be cowed at the mere whisper of the words "state secret"? The tactics of the Bush Administration are spreading like a plague, infecting judicial reasoning and hobbling courts everywhere. The courts exist as a check on the executive branch, and if they do not stand independently, we will all take one step toward tyranny. This will be a regime in which the greatest terror comes from within our borders, clothed by Brooks Brothers, adorned with our flag on its lapel, and probably carrying a cross.

> The natural law remains for us to defend, even though we hired a government to do so for us.

The last line of defense on the road to tyranny is the class of intrepid people who stand up for their unalienable rights, the few wolves who recall that *we* created a federal government to protect our rights. *We* created a government of limited powers, and *we* wrote the Constitution that set those limits. *We* the people. And the natural law remains for *us* to defend, even though we hired a government to do so for us.

Why won't the government do what we hired it to do?

10

LOOK PATRIOTIC: YOUR GOVERNMENT IS WATCHING

The alarm clock goes off. You hit snooze a few times. Finally you drag yourself out of bed and shuffle to the shower. You go through the motions of the regular morning routine on autopilot. You're running late—as usual—so you grab your keys, run out the door, and on to work you go. You hop into the car, and your favorite song is just starting. You turn the radio up and head off. You stop at your local coffee shop and grab a latte. At work, someone holds the front door open for you and, as you cross the lobby, you catch the elevator just in time. You have a lunch meeting a few blocks away. It's a beautiful day, so you figure, *If I walk a few blocks, I can skip the gym after work.* After the meeting, the day is practically over, so you grab a drink with a few friends and then head home for the night. Sounds like a typical day in the land of the free, right?

It is a typical day. But would it seem so normal if someone were watching the whole thing on a monitor? Surveillance cameras are everywhere, and whether you realized it or not, *you were being watched.* From the red-light camera at the intersection that caught you rushing through a yellow light, to the surveillance camera inside the coffee shop, the security camera in the lobby of your office-building and the one that caught you tripping over that crack in the sidewalk as you walked to lunch, the eyes in the sky were watching your every move.

Walking down a street in Manhattan presents a near guarantee that someone is watching you, and not just passersby either, nor the people in the offices above. You are being observed by thousands of surveillance cameras on the city streets—and by whoever monitors them. A study conducted by the New York Civil Liberties Union between 1998 and 2005 revealed that the number of surveillance cameras, both privately owned and those operated by the government, increased fivefold within areas of Manhattan during the years of the study. For example, Greenwich Village and SoHo had 142 visible cameras in 1998, and just seven years later in 2005, they had 2,227.[1]

The hypothetical situation I just described is virtually identical to *New York Post* reporter Brad Hamilton's typical Tuesday. Brad encountered more than twelve cameras in less than twenty-four hours. From getting his morning coffee to traipsing through his office

> Greenwich Village and SoHo had 142 visible cameras in 1998, and just seven years later in 2005, they had 2,227.

lobby to renting his nightly movie, practically every move Brad made throughout his day was caught on tape.[2]

In our modern, technologically infested society, you are never truly alone. Throughout each day, dozens of strangers gaze down on you as you flirt with the Jamba Juice hottie, punch in your pin number at the ATM, and kiss your significant other. They are peering down your shirt as you stroll down the street. Every day there are more and more stories of people abusing the use of surveillance cameras in order to entertain themselves.

The sick part is that the culprits are those who reap the benefits of your high taxes with their scaled salaries, paid vacations, and overtime pay.[3] They are the ones you pay to protect and serve you. That's right; the culprits are the police.

THE NYPD THOUGHT POLICE

The NYPD has been pushing the limits of video surveillance ever since September 11th. When groups of protesters convene, the police immediately send in their personal paparazzi to record the protestors' every move. The NYPD sends in moles pretending to be protestors. There are accounts of officers waving protest signs, holding flowers with mourners, riding bicycles in demonstrations, and some even wearing buttons stating, "I am a shameless agitator," while carrying a camera and videotaping the other protesters. Other incidents include a sham arrest of an undercover policeman, an incident which served as a catalyst for violence between police in riot gear and bystanders.[4]

Police spokesman Paul J. Browne said that "disguised officers have always attended such gatherings—not to investigate political activities, but to keep order and protect free speech." (When did the police suddenly become interested in anyone's freedom of speech but their own?) However, if that were the case, how can Browne explain the sham arrests? Were the police not clearly agitating the crowd? The actions of the NYPD were undoubtedly intended to stir up trouble to be able to capture the faces of the protesters on their little handheld video cameras.[5]

THE NYPD—OUR NEW "BODY" GUARDS?

On August 27th 2004, the NYPD was supposed to be videotaping a mass bicycle rally scheduled before a session of the RNC.

However, filming people riding their bikes must have gotten too mundane for these thrill-seeking officers, who turned the cameras off of the bikers and onto a rooftop high above Second Avenue. The camera's thermal-imaging equipment was able to capture a couple during an intimate moment they shared under the mistaken impression that they were hidden by the high walls and shrubs on the roof. The helicopter they heard overhead was videotaping them, and not the rally on the streets below.

"Aviation routinely checks and sometimes videotapes rooftop activity when someone's in a position to throw projectiles at the officers below," said police spokesman Paul J. Browne. So, the voyeur cops were not concerned with protecting the folks on the sidewalks and streets, or even the Republicans in Madison Square Garden, just filming sexual acts and claiming this somehow protects the cops. The air patrol was eventually instructed to terminate taping once it was determined a threat did not exist. Come on! With all this high-tech equipment, it still took a trained police officer four full minutes to determine that this amorous couple was not attempting to throw projectiles off the roof?[6] At the very least, the police would have violated "peeping tom" laws in numerous states, such as Vermont, Louisiana, and Arizona. Not to mention federal[7] and state video voyeurism laws that have been enacted in dozens of states,[8] including New York. New York's statute, now named "Stephanie's Law," prohibits the use of unlawful surveillance when someone intentionally uses "an imaging device to surreptitiously view, broadcast or record . . . the sexual or other intimate parts of such person at a place and time when such person has a reasonable expectation of privacy, without a person's knowledge or consent."[9] But these officers were not charged under Stephanie's Law, because sheep never accuse their shepherd.

WHAT GOES AROUND COMES AROUND

Just like wild animals, given the chance, the NYPD will even turn on its own. In the summer of 2004, the Patrolman's Benevolent Association, the union that represents the NYPD, organized a rally to protest the snail's pace of the contract negotiations with the City of New York. When the demonstrating NYPD officers arrived, they were herded into pens and stopped from handing out fliers. Fellow officers threatened to arrest them for standing on public sidewalks. Meanwhile, officers with a special videotaping unit captured images of all of the officers who turned against the City.

> **Why have you never heard of the officers speaking out against these tactics when they were the ones behind the video cameras?**

Isn't it ironic that the protesting officers found themselves subjected to their own intrusive, heavy-handed tactics? To take this insanity one step further, the officers are now suing the City and stating that the police procedures were *too* heavy-handed and violated their First Amendment rights. The officers might be right, but why have you never heard of the officers speaking out against these tactics when *they* were the ones behind the video cameras?[10]

AIN'T WORTH MUCH

Although surveillance cameras may be helpful in identifying the culprit after a crime has been committed, and they can be wonderfully incriminating in a court room, they hardly ever prevent a tragedy from happening. Just look at the 2005 subway bombings in London. This act of terrorism was carried out even though the UK has more surveillance cameras than any other country; over four million monitor the streets, government buildings, subways, and parks.[11] All the cameras were able to do was show us the steps the terrorists took before they killed so many innocent people. *The surveillance cameras did not stop a single attack.*

DON'T PICK YOUR NOSE IN PUBLIC . . .

As if cameras everywhere were not enough, those who watch the cameras are what make this invasion of privacy truly daunting. Some people cannot control their inner child, and if the opportunity presents itself, they can't say no to the temptation to goof off. From police officers to school personnel to casino employees, if there is a camera that can be manipulated or misused, someone will do it.

When you send your child off to school for the day, you are entrusting the school employees with the responsibility of keeping your child safe. Unfortunately, some are not as trustworthy as you might hope. At the Livingston Middle School in Overton County, Tennessee, cameras captured students between the ages of ten and fourteen in the boys' and girls' locker rooms at various stages of undress. The images were stored on a hard drive in the assistant principal's office, where they were remotely accessible.

The images were reportedly accessed ninety-eight times between July 2002 and January 2003 and through Internet providers in Clarksville, Tennessee; Gainesboro, Tennessee; and Rock Hill, South Carolina, sometimes late at night and in the wee hours of the morning.[12]

At another school, in Rolling Meadows, Illinois, a custodian was fired based on footage from a hidden camera in the teachers' lounge that revealed that he exceeded his break time.[13]

If the foul odor and sticky floors don't deter you from using public restrooms, you should be aware that they are probably more public than you might like. Cameras are frequently installed for security reasons in hotel bathrooms, toy stores, public parks, and even your local watering hole.[14]

Casino employees in Atlantic City, New Jersey, and Fort McDowell, Arizona, were caught taking advantage of their posts at security stations by manipulating the cameras to film female patrons and coworkers' breasts and buttocks.[15] And if you think these folks are unprofessional, the NYPD's Video Interactive Patrol Enhancement Response (VIPER) unit is far worse.

TREACHEROUS VIPERS

City Councilman Hiram Montserrate, himself a retired NYPD officer once assigned to the VIPER unit said, "Some stuff I witnessed was . . . clearly inappropriate use of the cameras in their surveillances—whether they were looking into people's windows or some of the male police officers looking at women. Clearly that is disturbing."[16] What was he talking about?

Since it is frowned upon to surf the Internet for porn while at work, some VIPER officers take advantage of the perks of their job and divert surveillance cameras to capture people having sex.

> VIPER officers take advantage of the perks of their job and divert surveillance cameras to capture people having sex.

In Sarah Wallace's exclusive exposé on the VIPER unit for WABC-TV New York, Sergeant John Marchisotto claims he saw a supervisor use the tenants in a nearby housing project for his entertainment. Sergeant Marchisotto said, "He [the supervisor] was showing a couple of cops that were working for him a video of two people having sex in the stairwell. Getting kicks out of watching residents of the housing development having sex."[17] Who will protect us from those we have hired to protect us?

A grisly suicide video of Paris Lane, a young, aspiring rapper, appeared on a porn Web site under the deranged title "Introducing: The Self-Cleansing Housing Projects." The video captures the last few moments of Lane's short life. He kissed his girlfriend good-bye, and she walked into the elevator. The elevator started going up, and a split second later, Paris pulled out a gun, stuck it in his mouth, and pulled the trigger. The most twisted part of this sad story is that the video came from cameras monitored by the NYPD's anticrime VIPER unit. Putting the pieces together, Lane's lawyer, Chris Robinson, said that only a VIPER police officer or a computer technician working for the City could have posted the horrifying video.[18]

These are just the renegade "bad cops," right? Well, yes. But unfortunately they comprise practically the entire VIPER unit. Wallace's WABC-TV exposé revealed that most of the cops in the VIPER unit (including some supervisors) monitoring the tapes had been ordered to modified duty, meaning they themselves have been involved in shootings or other criminal activity and are facing disciplinary or criminal charges. Also, the tapes are not safeguarded and are very easy to access, which would explain how the gruesome Paris Lane suicide video made it onto the Internet. And regarding formal training and procedures to monitor the surveillance tapes—there are none.[19]

LIGHTS, CAMERA, ACTION

In Tuscaloosa, Alabama, a traffic camera's angle was diverted from the intersection to the adjacent sidewalks to focus on pedestrians, particularly the young women from the University of Alabama. The footage, which was broadcast on citywide cable TV, showed the camera actually zooming in on the low-cut shirts and short skirts of the female students. As if this abuse of technology weren't enough, an officer on his dinner break saw the footage on TV and called headquarters to send officers to that location because *there was money to be made.* Three people were arrested and charged with a combination of public lewdness, disorderly conduct, public intoxication, and resisting arrest.[20] Why weren't the *cops* brought up on ethics charges?

EYES IN THE SKY

It has been statistically proven that the use of red light cameras (RLCs) and speed cameras increases the number of accidents that occur on the road. The District of Columbia installed the first RLC in 1999, and a study five years into the program revealed that the total number of broadside accidents increased by 30 percent, and the number of crashes that involved an injury or fatality rose 81 percent. In fact, these camera-ridden intersections often have worse accident statistics than intersections without cameras because drivers have a tendency to race through an intersection to beat the camera; an unthinkable act were a cop physically present.[21]

Officials across the country claim that one of the main reasons for the RLCs is safety. Yet it is hard to accept that explanation, considering that the statistics from around the nation show the exact opposite: RLCs increase the number of accidents at intersections. Sadly, this is not stopping states and municipalities from installing and keeping the cameras. After all, what politician cares about safety when the RLCs generate millions in revenue from traffic tickets, and all the municipality has to do is sign on the dot-ted line? The RLC manufacturers are responsible for every aspect of the program, in exchange for a cut of the revenue.

Although statistics show that cameras failed to reduce accidents, the City of Providence, Rhode Island, intends to add even more cameras to the City streets for "safety reasons." Want to guess why? The RLCs are expected to generate $1.9 million in revenue for the fiscal year, and as of April 2007, the program has already issued $648,825 in tickets. Affiliated Computer Services (ACS) runs this program for a cut of its revenue. "In most instances, the private company responsible for the cameras gets a 'kickback' for every ticket issued," Rhode Island lawyer Steven Brown stated, adding that "it is thus in their best interest—as well as the City's—to have people running red lights."[22]

It seems that some states are coming around. The Minnesota Supreme Court recognized that the use of red light cameras violates state law—which requires uniformity of traffic laws across the state—because the photo ticket program offered the accused fewer due process protections than the tickets received from an actual officer. The court also struck down the "rebuttable presumption doctrine." This is a prosecutor-generated rule that presumes that the driver of the photographed car is the registered owner. The driver should be "innocent until proven guilty." In the State of Minnesota, this was not always so: "The city [of Minneapolis] automatically presumed their guilt in a citation . . . The lower court judge agreed and ordered a halt to automated ticketing in Minneapolis."[23] Still, nationwide, the burden is on the owner of the vehicle to prove that he was not driving the vehicle at the time the photograph was taken.

Speed cameras perch atop overpasses and road signs along

> **Speed cameras have proved to be so profitable that in Britain they are referred to as "yellow vultures" and are the most lucrative cameras in the country.**

highways across the United States and Britain. The cameras are strategically spaced; the first of the two cameras takes an image of a car, and, when the same car passes the second camera, the numbers are crunched. The cameras calculate how long it took the car to get from point A to point B and then average the speed. If the average speed is over the designated speed limit, the owner of the car will receive a ticket in the mail, complete with the images to prove the driver's guilt. The tickets are practically indisputable, since the images of the vehicle are not close enough to capture the driver of the vehicle. If the license plate recorded is registered to you, you're guilty. Period. These cameras have proved to be so profitable that in Britain they are referred to as "yellow vultures" and are the most lucrative cameras in the country.[24]

DON'T MESS WITH TEXAS . . . OR MANHATTAN

In Texas, the State was not happy with local municipalities receiving the revenue from these "yellow vultures" and ordered the town of Marble Falls to remove its speed camera van from State highways, citing safety concerns. Recent legislation, however, only prohibits municipalities, like Marble Falls, from installing speed cameras; the bill does not prohibit the *State* from installing the same exact cameras.

We have not only emulated Britain with the use of "yellow vultures," but license-plate-reading cameras are also coming to the USA. License plate readers are cameras that check license plate numbers and send out an alert if a suspect plate is detected. These readers will be installed in fixed and mobile locations throughout Lower Manhattan in an attempt to resemble London's Ring of Steel.[25]

GREED AND THE NEED FOR SPEED

When it comes to generating income for their state or town, government officials have a hard time turning down the dough. Arizona's governor, Janet Napolitano (she is *not* my sister), plans on installing speed cameras on every major freeway within Arizona. The cameras currently on Loop 101 have generated over $5 million this year alone, and it is estimated that by the end of June 2007, revenue will top $7.5 million!

Revenue-producing schemes by local municipalities have been frowned upon within the judicial community. As long ago as 1927, the Supreme Court of the United States decided *Tumey v. Ohio*, in which it recognized the truism that judges and other law enforcement officials were more likely to find a person guilty when the conviction would increase their salaries and budgets. The Court ruled against the municipality, because Tumey was not able to receive a fair trial, which violated his Fourteenth Amendment right of due process. The legality of RLCs is questionable, especially regarding the revenue they generate for their local municipalities. If the courts follow the *Tumey* precedent, in a few years RLCs might simply be a sentence or two in history books. However, given the direction the herd has been grazing, it is unlikely that RLCs will go away anytime in the near future.

> As long ago as 1927, the Supreme Court recognized the truism that judges and other law enforcement officials were more likely to find a person guilty when the conviction would increase their salaries and budgets.

SLIDING DOWN THE SLIPPERY SLOPE

The larger issue regarding all of the RLCs, speed cameras, and license-plate-reading cameras is that Americans are just sitting back and accepting these everyday invasions of privacy. Why do we complacently allow the presumption of *guilt* and pay the fines simply because a hidden camera caught us speeding? Are we truly so malleable that we will conform our conduct to the understanding that our government is monitoring every move we make as part of our daily life?

Now that being constantly monitored is the norm, we are no longer outraged when we receive tickets in the mail because we didn't slam on our brakes at that yellow light, even if our experience and judgment informed us that it was safer to run the light than slam on the brakes and risk a rear-end collision. RLCs and their speed camera counterparts are slowly making the phrase "innocent until proven guilty" extinct and are destroying our ability to exercise our own judgment concerning safety and caution. Run a red light? Strict liability; no defenses.

If the government can presume guilt for traffic offenses by sending you the proof in the mail, how long will it be before the courts allow this to happen in more serious instances? Will people submissively acknowledge and pay the fines they receive in the mail simply because a camera claims they drove recklessly? Or what about accepting guilt because, to the lens of a camera, it appeared that you assaulted someone on the street, when actually it was just a funny angle. The burden is now on you to prove that you are innocent. This is not what our Founding Fathers envisioned.

For the sheep of the world, installing cameras everywhere is as natural as being counted at bedtime. After terrorist acts and violent crimes, such as September 11th and the Virginia Tech massacre, the sheep are content with surrendering their freedoms for the promise of security. But would they be so complacent if it weren't for the fear propagated by the footage of the tragedy played on a loop on every TV channel? It is a vicious cycle: Surveillance cameras are installed; violent acts are caught on tape; the tape is aired on the nightly news; the sheep are more terrified and want more cameras installed, so they can feel even more secure.

For all of the flashy "caught on tape" news segments, a majority of the captured footage is noncriminal and mundane. But this has not stopped the implementation of surveillance cameras. Even when cameras do not meet expectations, as is the case with the RLCs and safety concerns, they will continue to be installed. It seems that as long as people believe their safety is at risk, the sheep do not mind being watched.

If you still feel safer because your neighborhood is laden with surveillance cameras, take the advice of William S. Sessions. He was the Director of the FBI under Presidents Ronald Reagan, George H. W. Bush, and Bill Clinton. He has argued forcefully that cameras give us all, police and non-police, a false sense of safety when, in fact, "there is little evidence that these cameras are truly effective in preventing violent crime, and the potential damage done to individual liberty in these communities is immeasurable." He points out that even in Britain, "the cameras have no effect on violent crime."

There is no substitute for the cop on the beat; and if we appeal to the laziness of cops, who prefer not to walk a dangerous beat, we do so at the peril of our safety and our liberty.[26]

11

EVERYDAY LIFE AS A SHEEP

We are unaware of the many ways in which the government invades and scrutinizes our everyday lives. The massive government contracts for the development of shocking new technology for our ballooning security industry have proliferated at such a speed that it is no longer possible for the average person to stay reasonably informed. Some of the advances are classified, and some are state secrets. But the worst are those that we know about and tolerate on a daily basis. The first topic explored in this chapter is one with which we are all familiar, and have taken too lightly, as it affects our personal lives, our careers, our economy, and even our dignity.

AIRPORT SECURITY

Why is it that we surrender our water bottles and take off our shoes at the airport security counter? Why should we tolerate the slow, ineffective, and invasive screening process that has become a part of everyday life since September 11th? What is the Transportation Security Administration (TSA), and to whom is it accountable?

The government cannot constitutionally seize property without letting you first challenge the seizure in court and without paying you just what the property is worth. The Fifth Amendment to the Constitution guarantees that. Yet the list of forbidden items grows daily at airports throughout the United States, incredible and inane blunders by the TSA allow shocking breaches of security and raise the stakes for would-be travelers. These intrusions into our vacations and business trips would be less offensive if they were based on necessity and a rational, defensible scheme for protecting our security. But how does confiscating water bottles, snow globes, and "toy transformer robots" while waving deadly weapons and diseases through the gates, protect our security? How effective is a list of five hundred thousand suspected domestic terrorists in actually thwarting terrorism?

> Gel-filled bras and fluids with medical uses (including, specifically, K-Y Jelly) are exempt from the three-ounce limit imposed on most fluids at the security gates. The TSA's lists go into bizarre detail, permitting sabers and meat cleavers, for example, in checked luggage, but prohibiting water.

The list of items forbidden by the TSA changes daily; it is a testament to the ad hoc and often mystifying nature of the program. At the time of this writing, gel-filled bras and fluids with medical uses (including, specifically, K-Y Jelly) are exempt from the three-ounce limit imposed on most fluids at the security gates. The TSA's lists go into bizarre detail, permitting sabers and meat cleavers, for example, in checked luggage, but prohibiting water. Hand grenades and gunpowder are not allowed—even in checked baggage. The TSA explicitly permits children to bring "toy transformer robots" on board, in both carry-on and checked bags. Woe betide the TSA agent who stands between a child and his robots. But I have seen TSA agents seize an infant's bottle of milk at the gate. Games trump nourishment, I guess.

The *Seattle Times* has compiled a searchable database of many of the TSA's flagrant abuses of power. Not surprisingly, many of the incidents at the airport security gates go unreported. But some of the worst screwups make the press, and they include one college student's experiments with outwitting those we have hired to protect us.

NAUGHTY NATHANIEL

Nathaniel Heatwole, a twenty-year-old student at Guilford College in Greensboro, North Carolina, wasn't convinced that all the long lines, shoe scanning, and parched plane rides were actually doing anything to prevent terrorism in the air. Nathaniel took the initiative to test the security system. He attempted to smuggle items resembling a bomb-making kit and a box cutter through the gates.

In spite of the TSA's claims of safety and meticulousness, Heatwole succeeded. Three more times, at three different airports, Heatwole boarded with his bomb kits, nonchalantly passing through the gates at airports in Raleigh and Baltimore. He even had the presence of mind and diligence to e-mail the TSA, highlighting its faults in a letter that went ignored for nearly a month. In fact, Nathaniel Heatwole escaped charges until his bomb kits were discovered on several planes.[1] Heatwole is currently awaiting trial for carrying a concealed weapon aboard an aircraft. Meanwhile, he is banned from traveling by air and from visiting airports.

CHINKS IN THE ARMOR

In 2003, five employees of the Department of Homeland Security proved the TSA both fallible and incompetent. The mock "terrorists" set out to test the gates at Logan International Airport in Boston. They brought a carry-on bag containing knives, a gun, and a bomb through security, passing an X-ray machine and inspectors operating a metal detector. The carry-on made it onto the airplane without a hitch. The Mission Impossible team used bags that fit in the overhead compartment.

Logan Airport has upgraded its security measures in response to a recent alleged terrorist plot at JFK Airport, but the effectiveness of the changes remains to be seen. If it's so easy to bring weapons on a plane, maybe all that the rest of us need to do is to tuck our contraband moisturizer and Gatorade into our carry-ons before we reach the security counters. If we can hide our drinks and cosmetics a little better, at least we won't be parched when the passenger next to us sets off his government-approved bomb.

TB AND THE SUSPICIOUS SIPPY CUP

Perhaps the TSA would be able to stop weapons and explosives from getting through airport security if it weren't so focused on harmless, ordinary carry-on baggage. Consider the most recent scandal at Washington's Reagan National Airport, featuring an infant's sippy cup as the latest international threat.

On June 11th 2007, former Secret Service agent Monica Emmerson headed for the security gate at Reagan National, along with her nineteen-month-old son, to catch a flight to Reno, Nevada. Emmerson carried no restricted items, except for a child's cup, containing roughly four ounces of water. After inquiring whether the water was "nursery water"—a mysterious term absent from both TSA regulations and colloquial English—a TSA agent demanded that Emmerson leave the security area, empty the cup, and return, as her child wailed.

Emmerson refused to leave the area, allegedly calling the TSA program "stupid." Attempting to drink the offending "nursery water" herself, she spilled the cup as she removed its protective cover. A police officer made the former Secret Service agent clean up the water, on her hands and knees, as he threatened to arrest her for "endangering the public." Her fiancé and child watched as she was taken into custody by a total of four police officers and three TSA agents. She was interrogated and held for forty minutes. The family missed its flight to Nevada.

> A police officer made the former Secret Service agent clean up the water, on her hands and knees, as he threatened to arrest her for "endangering the public."

The TSA denies that its conduct was outrageous in any way. The deputy assistant administrator for security operations, Earl Morris, stated that "the allegation here that we were out of control is absolutely false." The TSA has since created a section on its Web site called "MythBusters" and posted footage of the incident with Emmerson that was captured on a nearby security camera. The video is unclear as to whether Emmerson spilled the cup intentionally or not. According to the TSA, the video does show that its "officers display professionalism and concern for all passengers."[2]

The TSA does not inspire confidence in our airport security. The feds ought to hire professional security agents and redefine its priorities to address legitimate threats rather than infants' water bottles. A wolf like Monica Emmerson makes this clear.

Worse still, the TSA does not have an excellent track record with *known* threats. In May 2007, officials at the Centers for Disease Control and Prevention in Atlanta, Georgia, discovered that a man from the United States was flying around the world with a rare, drug-resistant strain of tuberculosis.

The infected passenger was diagnosed with tuberculosis during a check-up in January. Five months later, he had been added to the "No Fly List," but he had not been detained or prevented from going on his honeymoon in Europe. Until he turned himself in to physicians at Bellevue Hospital in New York City, he was freer than the five hundred thousand other people on the No Fly List, many of whom are probably harmless or are on the list mistakenly, including Massachusetts Senator Ted Kennedy.

EVEN A *KENNEDY*?

Senator Kennedy mysteriously landed on the No Fly List as "T. Kennedy"—and had to call the Secretary of Homeland Security three times personally in order to get off it.

According to Kennedy, he took the security guard's actions lightly and asked an airport employee why he couldn't board the US Airways plane from Boston to Washington, on which he had been flying for forty-two years. A fair question. What kind of government blacklists one of its best-known senators, albeit one of its most prolific critics? Apparently, a suspected terrorist had traveled under Kennedy's name, landing the prominent surname on the No Fly List along with al-Qaeda members and people associated with other terrorist groups. It is also probable that Kennedy purchased a one-way ticket; a seemingly innocent activity that today raises red flags for the TSA watchdogs.

A VALET FOR VIPS?

What is the TSA doing about these debacles? As the embarrassing headlines pile up and our security seems weaker than ever, the Administration rolls out its newest innovation: looser restrictions for wealthy travelers!

VIPs, celebrities, businessmen, and government officials alike can now buy their way through security. Fliers who submit themselves to a background check and pay a fee can now enroll in varying levels of VIP security programs as "registered travelers" at airports such as Jacksonville International in Florida. The VIPs (silver, gold, or platinum, for example) get a shorter line at the security counter. They can keep their shoes on. And in some cases, they get valet parking, a separate lounge in the boarding area, and other perks, courtesy of this federally licensed program.[3]

SPINNING, SPINNING OUT OF CONTROL

Even if the unfairness of the program and the potential security threat that it poses don't bother you, consider the ever-expanding database of private information that the TSA is building on its travelers. True, travelers voluntarily submit their information in order to become VIPs, but it isn't clear how much information the Administration has gathered on the rest of us, or what it's doing with that information. The TSA claims to be taking our privacy seriously. But what about that hard drive that was mysteriously "lost," with confidential information on all of its employees? The TSA itself admits that data on some 100,000 people has been compromised, and there isn't anything that Homeland Security or the 180,000 employees there can do about it.

> The TSA itself admits that data on some 100,000 people has been compromised, and there isn't anything that Homeland Security or the 180,000 employees there can do about it.

Many people are only sensitive to these post-September 11th security issues when they're inside the airport gates. But sci-fi, government-funded, security technology is expanding beyond the endless check-in lines and into our daily lives. If we are not careful, we may wake up someday soon and discover that we are living in a truly Orwellian nightmare.

TECHNOLOGY IS NOT YOUR FRIEND

Security cameras, X-ray machines, wiretaps, phone records—all these invasions of privacy, and still government agents are not satisfied. They want to know what you eat, how you smell, what is in your saliva, how you walk, the topography of your face, and even your thermal plume (the halo of heat that surrounds you). If you think back to the most mind-blowing technology from your favorite sci-fi movie, it is likely that it is already in the development stages. In the near future, many of these technologies will be available, and Big Brother will have a plethora of tools at its disposal to track your every move. Does your spouse know you as well as the government will?

After September 11th, various means of identifying people quickly and efficiently in public places have been put on the developmental fast track. The company that develops these technologies first will reap the benefit of millions (if not billions) of dollars from American taxpayers. Although some of these technologies are still in their infancy, companies hoping for government contracts are accelerating these projects in order to take advantage of a nation living in fear.[4]

Software-defined radio is a fascinating yet scary new technology that captures the stray radiation emitted by all computers. The scanner records and translates the waves into duplicates of every image, document, and Web page that is accessed on the targeted computer's screen. So, where electronic surveillance of Internet use ends, software-defined radio surveillance picks up with a copy of every document opened and database used. And don't expect the government to get search warrants before it uses its newest intrusive techniques.

The U.S. Defense Advanced Research Projects Agency has funded projects that can identify a person by his or her gait. This is done by measuring the silhouette of a torso, the swinging of the shoulders and legs, and the time it takes to move through a single step. At this stage of the research, a woman in heels could still deceive the system, but there are certain signature rhythms that are more difficult to hide.[5]

Once scientists know how you move, they will also be able to know what makes up your scent. They are working on supersensors, which have the ability to pick molecules off of you that are released at very low concentrations that make up your individual scent. These molecules are then analyzed by a computer that generates your individual scent pattern.[6] Note to self: Don't forget the deodorant.

Scientists are scrambling to develop technology that will help identify you by your outer qualities, but what about what is inside of you? Your mouth and eyes are hotbeds for prying researchers. Dentists have been trying to find ways to identify persons by the ribonucleic acid (RNA) in their saliva.[7] And iris scans have already evolved tremendously. The Sarnoff Corporation has developed "Iris on the Move," which can scan up to twenty irises a minute while people are walking through an entryway.[8]

A little cover-up won't be able to hide your blemishes from Big Brother anymore. High-resolution cameras now allow face-recognition software to reach a whole new level. This software can analyze your skin by inspecting the size of your pores, wrinkles, and spots on your face. Some systems can even create a topographical map of your face using infrared light. And the government makes sure it will get a full shot of your face due to the various laws prohibiting masks and disguises in public places (even though it is perfectly legal for government agents to hide their identities).[9]

Although there is plenty of technology in the developmental stages, some outrageous new technology is already being used across the Atlantic. In the UK, security cameras not only capture images; they now can talk to you, too! Cameras in the town of Wirral, England, have been fitted with speakers that allow the police to reprimand people if they commit misdemeanors, such as littering and vandalizing property. Louise Casey,

> High-resolution cameras now allow face-recognition software to reach a whole new level. This software can analyze your skin by inspecting the size of your pores, wrinkles, and spots on your face.

the coordinator for the Respect Task Force (a government-initiated group that aims to tackle bad behavior and nurture good),[10] defended the latest incursion from the nanny state: "The new equipment will make an important contribution in reminding people about what is, and what is not, acceptable behavior and to think twice before acting anti-social [sic] again." Sounds great in theory, but have humans become such barbarians that they need a megaphone to yell at them when they are "anti-social"?[11] And what does "anti-social" mean? Whatever the current government bureaucrat in charge of the program wants it to mean.

The UK has also tested a radio frequency identification (RFID) tag. This tag was placed on fifty thousand volunteers to track their movements throughout an airport so that the airport can track the "efficiency" of its security. Since a missing passenger can cause chaos in a terminal (for example, forcing airlines to remove all baggage from the hold), this chip is intended to help airlines reduce delays and save money.[12]

True, there is no evidence that this technology is being used in the United States. At least not yet. But how long is the U.S. government really going to allow its island ally across the pond to use this nifty new technology without figuring out a way to claim it as our own and make it bigger, better, and more profitable? But could these new technologies, such as the RFID tag, be here already? Could they someday be implanted under our skin without us even consenting to it?

> Does the average person really need to be identified with the same mechanisms possibly used to protect our nation's most highly classified information?

This technology is obviously revolutionary, and it is quite astonishing how far we have evolved in order to create these new-age inventions. However, are they really necessary for the general population? Yes, technologies have their place in highly secured areas, such as the inner portions of the Pentagon and CIA headquarters, but aren't subway stations a bit unworthy of these pricey and intrusive technologies? Does the average person really need to be identified with the same mechanisms possibly used to protect our nation's most highly classified information?

MISSION "CREEPY"

Considering the government's history regarding our privacy with newly emerging technology, we are unlikely to regain any of our privacy; in fact, it is very possible that we will only lose more of it. *Mission creep* is the term coined to explain the tendency of government projects to slip silently beyond their original goal and hence the project's boundaries. According to a recent study, databases created for one purpose are almost inevitably used for another, not always legitimate, purpose.[13]

Former *New York Times* columnist William Safire was concerned about our privacy being stripped away years before we were fighting a "war on terror" and also offers us a prime example of mission creep. In 1998, Safire wrote about how Big Brother was watching as never before and that when you use E-ZPass to pay for tolls and credit cards to pay for groceries, the government has a detailed profile of information on you. It was considered outrageous at the time. Today in the post-September 11th world, the government is no longer *possibly* monitoring your credit card purchases; it *is* monitoring them. With one NSL, agents of the government can obtain anything about you, and it is legal. The government tracking your daily life is no longer just for the conspiracy theorists; it is a reality to which the sheep have lamentably become accustomed.

It is virtually impossible to regain your privacy; however, if you really want to maintain it, you must forgo some modern-day conveniences, such as e-mail and credit cards. "Cash is the enemy of intruders," because it is nearly impossible to track.[14] Consider the items you can't live without on a daily basis: your driver's license, your credit cards, your ATM card, your cell phone, your BlackBerry. From these everyday items, the government can learn nearly everything about your daily routine.

BIG BROTHER: JUST A *PING* AWAY

Besides the obvious fact that the government knows who you are calling and who is calling you (again, via NSLs), your phone also tracks your every move while it is turned on.[15] Authorities routinely use GPS tracking capabilities in cell phones to narrow the search area when looking for a missing person. Remember the Kim family, whose members got lost when they made a wrong turn while traveling through Oregon and got stuck in the snow? Rescue teams were able to narrow their search area because the Kims' cell phone emitted "pings" which eventually led to the rescue of Mrs. Kim and her two daughters; unfortunately, the rescuers were not in time to save Mr. Kim.[16]

> As long as you are carrying your phone, the government can easily find out where you are by following the pings and will probably be listening to your every word—even if your cell phone is off.

Although this seems like a revolutionary way to save mountain climbers lost in an avalanche and to locate runaway children, the potential for abuse of this technology is obvious. Think of the ways in which the government can, and probably already does, use this technology to track people whose thoughts, ideas, and words it hates and fears. As long as you are carrying your phone, the government can easily find out where you are by following the pings and will probably be listening to your every word—even if your cell phone is off. Our cell phones have become as essential to our daily lives as the oxygen we breathe; we cannot leave our homes without them, and when we do, we feel completely disconnected from our friends, family, and the rest of the world. Cell phone addiction has been a brilliantly executed plan because now we are addicted and feel naked without them. The government can use our cell phones as tracking devices and as microphones permanently attached to our belt loops and inside our handbags.

To some, highly sophisticated technology is a friend to privacy, because the more accurate the technology becomes, the less likely that people will be falsely identified.[17] Think back to second-grade math class: when you average only a few numbers that vary greatly, say 1 and 100, the average is not as accurate as when you average many numbers that are close together, say 1 through 10. The worst problems arise when each bit of information an individual gives up over the course of a day, from the PIN number he uses to buy his morning coffee to the Web sites he surfs at night, gets put into various databases that create a detailed profile of that innocent person's daily routine.[18] Just as when you average 1 and 100, the average (or profile, in this case) does not reflect the two numbers accurately.

PRIVACY IN PERIL

Databases don't only track your daily routine; they are also able to capture the essence of what makes you, well, *you*, through biometric measures such as your fingerprints, iris scans, and facial recognition software. However, the problem with biometrics is that the science is not black and white; there are large areas of gray. Data can be misinterpreted, and innocent people can be accused of heinous crimes. Brandon Mayfield, an Oregon lawyer who also just happened to convert to Islam, was falsely accused and imprisoned for two weeks because his fingerprints *partially* matched a fingerprint obtained in connection with the terrorist train bombings in Madrid, Spain.[19]

Your privacy will probably never be restored unless you cut yourself off from all technology. If we all just quit Googling everything and went back to the library, tossed out our BlackBerrys, and returned to the good old snail-mail system, then the government would have no data to mine. But they'd probably still read our mail.

Technology has become an integral part of our lives. And the progress of making our daily lives more convenient—by not having to be at your house to receive a phone call or at your office to check your e-mail—is regrettably perceived by many as worth the sacrifice of losing your privacy. But we need assurance that the collection and use of this data is being monitored responsibly.

YOU CAN'T TAKE THIS: IT'S MINE

Forget about privacy for a moment; what about property? The Constitution protects you from the government coming in and taking your property without paying you its fair value, right?

Wrong.

> If we all just quit Googling everything and went back to the library, tossed out our BlackBerrys, and returned to the good old snail-mail system, then the government would have no data to mine.

Thanks to the disastrously broad interpretation by the Supreme Court of the eminent domain clause of the Fifth Amendment, the government may take your land and your home if its use would provide a "public benefit." This loosely defined and poorly understood legal term is so malleable that as long as the local government can make some argument as to expected "benefits" to the community from the taking of the land, the recent Supreme Court ruling means that the government *can* take your land and your home, even if the land will be transferred to another private party.

The Supreme Court ruled that the City of New London, Connecticut, could take the private property of Suzette Kelo, raze the home that she and her family had lived in for generations, and sell the land to private developers, because the proposed use of the land would invigorate an economically depressed neighborhood and, thus, confer the "public benefit" of more tax dollars to the tax collector. That's a benefit?

The City was reacting to the possibilities provided by a newly built Pfizer plant. Seizing on the opportunity to boost earnings through taxes and create a prettier, more pristine neighborhood, it formed the New London Development Corporation to plan a hotel, residences, a park, and retail outlets in its Fort Trumbull area. This would've been a wonderful idea for the residents of New London, had the city not condemned their homes when those living in the development zone refused to sell to the Corporation. Fifteen home-owners fought against the City, and all of them lost their homes. The City initially valued the fifteen lots at $1.6 million collectively, or $107,000 each, which would be paid to the individual owners.

Legally the court's decision is not as noteworthy as the contro-versy that it has generated in the press. The Fifth Amendment to the Constitution provides that the government can seize private prop-erty *for public use*, as long as it fairly compensates the owner. The state has always been able to exercise eminent domain for public use; now it has merely changed that term of art to "public benefit." Perhaps the most disturbing aspect of the case is that the City seized property from one private citizen and sold it to another. There was no public use.

The public use requirement, combined with the "just compen-sation" requirement, serves to limit further the government's emi-nent domain power. This requirement ensures that the taking is legitimate. The government has no right to condemn your property and sell it to your neighbor, no matter how much it chooses to com-pensate you and no matter how much your neighbor compensates the government. Accordingly, the government has no authority to take your property, under any circumstances, no matter what it says, and no matter what it pays you, for a private use. For decades, however, courts have sidestepped the public "use" requirement with the rule that takings that indirectly "benefit" the public may also be considered "public uses."

> The government has no right to condemn your property and sell it to your neighbor, no matter how much it chooses to compensate you and no matter how much your neighbor compensates the government.

Public officials largely sympathized with those who lost their homes. The governor of Connecticut, M. Jodi Rell, offered them property in the Fort Trumbull area in exchange for the land that they lost. State governments (including Michigan, Ohio, Florida, and New Hampshire) are gradually implementing laws and amendments to their constitutions to limit the use of eminent domain in response to the *Kelo* case. Even President Bush has stepped into the debate, issuing an executive order on June 23rd 2006, forbidding the federal government to follow in the City of New London's footsteps.

The *Kelo* case represents a disturbing precedent in the law, but it also shows that those who refuse to be cowed by the government are not always beaten down. The mass of public sentiment favoring the homeowners in the Fort Trumbull area led to swift, nationwide government action in their support. If this is true of intrusive attempts on our very homes, it may also bode well for attempts on our privacy.

We could all learn from Suzette Kelo's response to the City of New London's abuse of eminent domain. The government's intrusions on American freedom and its flagrant disregard for our Constitution must stop somewhere; the government has tried to invade our privacy and our homes, and now it is trying to take them and literally demolish them. It has become a bandit that robs from the poor to give to the rich, a legion of thieves in sportcoats. It has gone too far, and we must do something about it.

12

THE CORPSE OF HABEAS

Picture this: It's Tuesday. You had a long day at work, and all you want to do is to relax and spend some quality time with your family. Just as the teapot begins to whistle, there is a fierce pounding on your front door. You look through the peephole and there are three large men in suits. Maybe you did something illegal; maybe you didn't. They threaten to break down the door if you don't open it. With shock and terror in their eyes, your children cower behind their mother, who has tears in her eyes as you are handcuffed, dragged out of the house, and thrown in the back of an armored vehicle.

You are transported to a military base and kept in confinement, without charge, without access to lawyers, and prohibited from contacting your family. You are subjected to both psychological and physical interrogation techniques. After a while, you are broken and defeated. You confess to whatever it is they say you've done just so that maybe, just maybe, they won't rape and torture your wife and kids, as they've been threatening to. Then they use your confession to sentence you to death.

Oh yeah, and you're white. You're an Irish Catholic who came to America for college and are living in the country legally. Let the outrage begin. Even the most loyal and "patriotic" Bush congregant

140

won't attempt to defend this blatant and severe violation of basic constitutional liberties. The international community is shocked and appalled. Every newspaper writes "This isn't Soviet Russia" editorials chastising the government's abuse of a legal alien's constitutional right to the writ of habeas corpus.

But, change the *Mc* or *O'* prefix to *al*, the religion to Islam, and the skin color to brown, and the exact same scenario barely hits the front page.

The guarantee of habeas corpus is the part of the Constitution that prevents the government from swooping in, under the cover of night, abducting us out of our beds and confining us in a cell for the rest of our lives, or even for a day, without ever knowing what we did or having the opportunity to compel the government to prove our guilt. It is the foundation of all other rights, because without it, we would have no right to challenge unlawful infringements upon our privacy, free speech, religion, and due process. It encompasses the rights that prevent us from living in a perpetual state of fear that our government could erase our existence if it decided to do so.

Unfortunately, the Bush Administration has employed its most maniacally brilliant legal minds to develop a way to avoid the confines of the Constitution and create a loophole in which it is immune from being charged with war crimes. What they came up with is an extrajudicial system that gives the executive branch exclusive power to decide that an individual is an "enemy combatant." Once designated as such, you are stripped of your habeas corpus rights; you can be whisked off to Gitmo and detained indefinitely without charge. If charges are eventually filed, the trial is heard before, not an impartial jury, but high-ranking military officers of the very government that captured you to begin with. Good luck getting access to independent civilian counsel, and forget about seeing the government's evidence against you.

The American people's utter lack of outrage over the unsubstantiated imprisonment of anyone potentially related to al-Qaeda or the Taliban amounts to an authorization of Islamic internment camps. Today, the federal government acts as if anyone of Middle Eastern descent or any follower of the Islamic faith is a potential suicide bomber or prodigy of Osama bin Laden.

> **Today, the federal government acts as if anyone of Middle Eastern descent or any follower of the Islamic faith is a potential suicide bomber or prodigy of Osama bin Laden.**

Sure, it may make scores of Midwestern white Protestants feel safer. But what about Middle Eastern Muslims?

If you like(d) President Bush and agree that terrorists don't deserve the same rights as law-abiding Americans, then maybe you don't see what the big deal is. Terrorists are bad. The problem is that the executive branch and its military tribunals have full authority to declare someone a terrorist and send that person into perpetual imprisonment without any evidence that he or she is in any way involved with "terrorist activities."

Some Americans don't have a problem with this, because they are still so hurt and angry about September 11th and harbor animosity toward Middle Eastern people in general. But "terror" is a vague and malleable thing to have a war against. If the present executive branch gets to decide who is a terrorist, what about the future enemies of future presidents?

Imagine (completely hypothetically) that we "win" the war on terror and suddenly peace and democracy are flourishing in the Middle East. A few years down the road, we have a new administration on Capitol Hill that actually respects the Constitution and takes seriously its oath to be bound by it. Then, an extremist group of disgruntled immigrants who were ejected back to squalid slums in Mexico City as a result of new immigration reform laws somehow manages to contaminate drinking water across America with a potent strain of the bacteria that pollutes the water they have been forced to drink all their lives. Hundreds of thousands of Americans across the country get violently ill. The hospitals and clinics and drug companies can't distribute medicine fast enough, and many die.

The president calls it "biological warfare" and declares the perpetrators terrorists. Suddenly there are riots and violence in cities across the country. Since a quarter of the U.S. population is comprised of people of Hispanic descent, whose families risked everything to come to America in search of a better life, many Hispanic Americans, citizens of the United States, sympathize with and even support the "terrorists." That is, these Hispanic Americans entertain thoughts with which the federal government disagrees.

Because of dangerous precedents set during the Bush Administration's war on terror, the future president could declare American citizens who support the immigrant uprising *with their silent thoughts* to be "enemy combatants" and ship them off by the truckload to Gitmo or one of the many large prison camps that would need to be built.

Does the word *gulag* ring any bells?

GITMO: A LEGAL BLACK HOLE

Since his inauguration, George W. Bush and the rest of his executive team have been hard at work developing a series of laws that allow them to run their "war" on their terms by avoiding the constraints of the Constitution and a variety of domestic and international laws prohibiting torture.

With the war on terror in full swing, the U.S. Government began shipping terrorism suspects and enemy combatants[1] to the naval detention camp in Guantánamo Bay, Cuba, commonly known as "Gitmo."

Gitmo was designed to be a legal black hole. Because it is outside of U.S. territory, the Bush team decided that Gitmo also operates independently of the U.S. rule of law. The Department of Defense invented the Guantánamo Military Commission, a tribunal composed of military personnel, to handle the trials of Gitmo detainees. Only the presiding officer of the five-member commission was required to be a lawyer. The military commissions did not operate according to the rules governing U.S. courts or the Uniform Code of Military Justice (the justice system for members of the U.S. military). Secluded from the scrutiny of the U.S. legal system, detainees were imprisoned indefinitely without charge and subjected to torturous interrogation techniques.

> Gitmo was designed to be a legal black hole. Because it is outside of U.S. territory, the Bush team decided that Gitmo also operates independently of the U.S. rule of law.

For three years Gitmo operated below the radar of much of the American public. Members of the legislative branch and the general public rallied behind the president's plan to rid the world of terrorism and sheepishly allowed the executive branch to declare unchecked authority to achieve that goal.

But in 2004, the wolves emerged from their shadows. Legal representatives for Yaser Esam Hamdi, a U.S. citizen by birth who was captured in Afghanistan in 2001 and held for three years without charge, succeeded in getting the Supreme Court to consider the legal conundrum at Gitmo.

In response to Hamdi's charges that he had been illegally deprived of his habeas corpus rights, the government claimed that it had the power to detain, indefinitely and without charge or any judicial oversight, any prisoners designated by a military commission as "enemy combatants." The Supreme Court said, "No way"—eight of the nine justices supported the Constitution by declaring that U.S. citizens, even if classified as "enemy combatants," may not be detained without basic due process protections (notice of charges, access to counsel, and a right to a speedy trial).

Following the *Hamdi v. Rumsfeld* decision, the wolves gained momentum, and the Gitmo policy quickly crumbled. In *Rasul v. Bush*, the Supreme Court rejected the government's argument that anyone held outside of U.S. territory is subject to the exclusive authority of the military commissions. It also held that U.S. federal courts have the authority to hear habeas corpus petitions filed by Gitmo detainees.

In 2006, the Court's *Hamdan v. Rumsfeld* decision seriously undermined the scope of unchecked executive authority. The Court's opinion focused on three crucial points. First, the president did not have the authority to convene the military commissions without the consent of Congress. Second, even if he possessed such power, the military commissions were illegal because of substantial deviations from laws of war—violating provisions of both the Uniform Code of Military Justice and the Geneva Conventions. Finally, the Court specifically held that, contrary to the decision handed down by the lower court (which, by the way, at the time of the *Hamdan* appeal, had as one of its members the future Bush-appointed Supreme

Court Chief Justice John G. Roberts Jr.), the Geneva Conventions do apply at Gitmo.

But the Supreme Court's blatant rejection of the military commission system that President Bush ordered on his own, and the Court's order to obey the Constitution and Geneva Conventions did not deter the Bush Administration. The strategy team went back to the drawing board and drafted a new plan to salvage their above-the-law ideas.

The result was the Military Commissions Act of 2006 (MCA06). Although several amendments were proposed before final passage of the bill—including one that would terminate the authority of the Act after five years; another that would have prohibited specific interrogation techniques, including waterboarding; and one that would have preserved habeas corpus—all were defeated. The bill passed in both houses of Congress and was signed into law by President Bush in October 2006.[2]

MCA06 essentially purports to negate all of the Supreme Court's decisions with Congressional approval. I say "purports" because it is very difficult—indeed the instances are rare and the success rate is dismal—for the Congress by ordinary legislation to overrule or supplant a Supreme Court decision on the meaning of rights guaranteed by the Constitution. But Congress tried to do so with MCA06. It gives the president exclusive authority to convene the military commissions. It specifically exempts the military commissions from following the Uniform Code of Military Justice's habeas corpus provisions and UCMJ precedent in general. Enemy combatants are exempt from the Geneva Convention protections against torture and inhumane treatment.[3]

MCA06 gives the military commissions exclusive jurisdiction over unlawful enemy combatants. A Combatant Status Review

Tribunal "or another tribunal established under the authority of the President or Secretary of Defense" decides whether a prisoner is an unlawful enemy combatant.[4] The bill defines unlawful combatants as *anyone* who has "engaged in hostilities, or purposefully and materially supported hostilities against the United States."[5] So, anyone a tribunal convened by the president decides has "materially supported hostilities" against the United States may be detained indefinitely without charge at Gitmo and has no right to challenge the detention in the U.S. courts. And if the "support" was mental in nature only, you, my dear reader, can lose your freedom because of your thoughts: no charges, no judge, no lawyer, no trial, no witness, no evidence. Just permanent punishment because of *what the president claims are your illegal thoughts.*

This statute leaves open some ominous possibilities. Didn't the president himself say, "You're either with us or you're with the terrorists"?[6] Does that mean that American citizens who donate to antiwar organizations are supporting hostilities? What about American Muslims who donate to their mosques? What about heroin junkies? Their money is supporting the opium trade in Afghanistan, which funds the Taliban. With the potential for a perpetual war on terror and the sweeping language of MCA06, the limits on who can be labeled an enemy are as nonexistent as the boundaries of the battlefield.

Fortunately, while planning the parallel military justice system they designed to reign over Gitmo, the Bush team neglected to consider the fact that military lawyers and judges are bound by two competing codes: (1) the code of the U.S. Armed Forces to protect and serve the country and its values; and (2) the ethical code of the legal profession that will not allow them to ignore the Constitution, the law, or participate in wild, bizarre applications of it.

The reviews to determine enemy combatant status were done prior to the passing of the MCA06 (where the lawful vs. unlawful distinction became the determinant of whether the case can be heard in federal courts or is under exclusive jurisdiction of the military commissions). As a result, the detainees are classified as "enemy combatants" only, which means that, technically, they are not under the jurisdiction of the military commissions.

Two separate military judges in two separate hearings of the only prisoners to make it to trial before the military commissions at Gitmo refused to ignore the distinction between "lawful" and "unlawful" enemy combatants. Both cases were dismissed for lack of jurisdiction. The least they could have done is call and give a heads-up to the White House so they could have claimed the state secrets privilege and prevented the press from being there to witness the massacre on the executive ego. Damn insubordinate judges!

It appears there are two options: either the charges must be dropped against all detainees and their cases transferred to the federal courts, or every case must be re-reviewed by a Combatant Status Review Tribunal to determine whether each detainee is properly detained as an enemy combatant and whether he is classified as lawful or unlawful within the meanings in the Military Commissions Act. Although the military commissions are proving to be a cumbersome failure, if their track record is any indicator, you can bet the White House will be pushing for the latter. Wait a minute. Can a detainee whose status has been determined as a lawful enemy combatant—as our captured uniformed soldiers and sailors were in our declared wars—actually be tried over and over again until the government gets the result it wants? Answer: Under MCA06, yes, even though the Constitution expressly forbids this practice (called "double jeopardy").

THE ENEMY COMBATANT CONUNDRUM

In December 2001, Ali al-Marri, a citizen of Qatar who had lawfully entered the United States with his wife and five children, was arrested at his home in Peoria, Illinois, as a material witness to the government's investigation of the September 11th attacks. Al-Marri was charged with intent to commit credit card fraud and awaited criminal trial in civilian jail. Even though he spent his time in America in Illinois, and even though none of the September 11th hijackers did, the government claimed he was a material witness against them. Less than one month before his trial date, al-Marri was declared an enemy combatant by President George W. Bush himself. Without any hearing or explanation of the evidence against him, al-Marri was suddenly transferred into military custody.

He was held in military confinement without charge for four years. For the first sixteen months, al-Marri was kept incommunicado; he wasn't even permitted to contact his lawyers. He was deprived of basic necessities and subjected to inhumane and degrading interrogation methods. Agents of your government told him they'd rape his wife if he did not confess to aiding the September 11th conspiracy.

Finally, with the assistance of vehement constitutional advocates, a federal court has defied the political pressures of Washington and delivered a crucial decision in the fight to save our constitutional rights. The court concluded that the president does not have the authority to declare civilians, even a civilian against whom the government has filed criminal charges, legally residing in the United States, to be "enemy combatants" and strip them of their habeas corpus rights indefinitely.

"To sanction such presidential authority to order the military to seize and indefinitely detain civilians," Judge Diana Gribbon Motz wrote for the majority opinion, "even if the president calls them 'enemy combatants,' would have disastrous consequences for the Constitution—and the country."[7]

FAUX JUSTICE

If the Combatant Status Review Tribunal actually does an investigation and determines that a particular detainee is an unlawful enemy combatant, and the government does decide to file charges, then comes the yet-untested Military Commission trial. Although loosely modeled on the U.S. court system, MCA06 provides for some startling departures that make the possibility of a "fair trial" unlikely.

Given that the secretary of defense has exclusive authority to appoint judges and change or remove them at any time based on "competence to perform,"[8] obviously the independence and impartiality of a military judge is compromised, to put it mildly.

On top of facing biased judges, a detainee may only be represented by nonmilitary-appointed counsel if he or she[9] has been determined to be eligible for access to classified information.[10] Eligibility for access to classified information may be granted only to United States citizens for whom an investigation has been completed and whose personal and professional history indicates unquestioned allegiance and loyalty to the United States.[11]

Whether the lawyer is military or civilian probably won't matter anyway, since neither will be able to build a defense. The MCA06 has a broad "National Security Privilege" clause that allows the government to prevent disclosure of information that could be "detrimental to the national security."[12] This is especially problematic because MCA06 authorizes the government to use hearsay ("I heard from a tribesman in northern Afghanistan that the defendant plotted against the United States") and statements obtained from the accused through coercive and torturous techniques (which an FBI agent personally confirmed to me during a visit to Gitmo did take place during Gitmo's first few years of operation) as "evidence" in the accused's trial—practices that are strictly outlawed under U.S. law.

The government can base its entire case on a confession culled from the accused after being chained naked to a wall for days in extreme temperatures, urinating and defecating on himself while the guards desecrate his holy book by flushing it down a toilet. And if in the process of the torture he mentions a name that he heard might have some involvement with terrorism, that guy will probably be convicted too. The defense can't challenge the accuracy of any admissions or confessions because the sources, methods, and activities by which evidence against the accused was acquired are all classified. Even if the government fabricated the evidence entirely, the defense would have no way of proving it.

But, if by some miracle the accused is able to prove his innocence and is acquitted on all charges, then the nightmare will finally be over. The government will publicly apologize for the grave mistake and reward the detainee millions in damages for wrongful imprisonment and emotional injury—Oh, wait! I got confused there for a second. That's what happens in *actual* justice systems. Under MCA06, once Gitmo detainees are designated as "unlawful enemy combatants," they are exempt from habeas corpus rights. So if the military commission trial finds that the detainment of the accused was completely unfounded, that there is no evidence that he did anything to support terrorism in any way, there is still no guarantee that he will be released! In fact, under the MCA06, the president could detain the *acquitted, innocent* defendant for as long as the president wishes.

Most of the sheep are contented by President Bush's constant reminders of how "evil" the terrorists are. They have been lulled into a false sense of security that rounding up the "evildoers" and throwing them into a prison in the middle of the ocean will somehow make the sheep safer. What the sheep don't understand is that, thanks to MCA06, if a new and even more dangerous shepherd decides that *they* are a threat, they could very easily be next.

13

TORTURE: DON'T ASK, DON'T TELL, DON'T TOUCH

As an American, I am embarrassed and enraged that more people are not infuriated about the heinous abuse of basic civil liberties and human rights of prisoners at Gitmo and in the secret CIA prisons around the world. But the sheep are not entirely to blame for their ambivalent complacence. The government has gone to great lengths to keep the drastic and alarming perversions of power hidden from public scrutiny.

But even when the information is widespread and available, many Americans would rather change the channel and distract themselves with the contrived drama of reality TV than consider the actual reality that their own government could behave in a manner so criminal, brutal, hypocritical, and unconstitutional. We want to believe that we are the inheritors and preservers of freedom and democracy. We want to trust that our government obeys its own laws. It's just easier that way. The sheep don't want to take time out from lazily grazing in their coach potato pastures to consider the turmoil outside the flock.

The simple fact that Americans are too distracted by celebrity gossip, video games, and sports and are too preoccupied with acquiring massive amounts of stuff, to notice that their government is dissolving their liberties and committing crimes in their name, has turned out to be quite convenient for the Bush Administration.

As soon as the first group of accused terrorists reached Gitmo, shattering the limits on interrogation techniques became the pet project of Vice President Cheney. The Justice Department's Office of Legal Counsel, including the vice president's general counsel, David S. Addington, and his colleague, John C. Yoo, the likely original authors of the now-infamous "torture memo," went to work reinterpreting the law and translating theories of executive supremacy into a novel legal approach to wartime authority.

The torture memo advised the president that he could declare that the prisoner-of-war protections of the Geneva Conventions[1] do not apply to al-Qaeda, Taliban fighters, or other prisoners in the war on terror. Thus, according to the memo's theory, the prohibitions against the use of violent, cruel, inhumane, humiliating, and degrading treatment are obsolete. Instead, the memo suggested a general direction to adhere to humane treatment "to the extent appropriate and consistent with military necessity."[2]

The Addington/Yoo torture memo advised President Bush that the government did not have to comply with the standard interpretations of international treaties, including the Geneva Conventions, and could decline to enforce the federal War Crimes Act, enacted by a Republican Congress and signed into law by President Clinton in 1996,[3] and instead could accept a new legal framework that was designed to allow room for extremely cruel interrogation methods without fear of prosecution for the commission of war crimes.

When the memo was presented to the president (via then White House Counsel Alberto Gonzales), he adopted its ambiguous and malleable language verbatim. The memo concluded, and the

Ashcroft Justice Department agreed, that in order for an act to constitute torture, it must inflict physical pain "equivalent in intensity to the pain accompanying serious physical injury, such as organ failure, impairment of bodily function, or even death."[4]

Of course, all of this language in the torture memo was declared by President Bush to be strictly classified information. In April 2004, the horrifying images of the humiliation and torture of inmates by U.S. soldiers at Abu Ghraib prison in Iraq were revealed by the media. The president framed it as an isolated incident, a "failure of character" of this select group of soldiers. Seven soldiers were court-martialed and forced to bear the blame for a policy that the White House had approved.

The torture memo was shocking proof that the president had knowingly authorized cruel, inhumane, and criminal treatment of detainees that would qualify as war crimes under federal and international law. The resulting public outcry led Congress to enact the Detainee Treatment Act of 2005, which included the Geneva Conventions' protections against torture.

> **The torture memo was shocking proof that the president had knowingly authorized cruel, inhumane, and criminal treatment of detainees that would qualify as war crimes under federal and international law.**

But with a few tweaks of the language, the policy slipped through with congressional approval as part of the Military Commissions Act of 2006.[5] While the MCA06 does not specifically endorse torture, it does make those dubbed "enemy combatants" immune from the protections of the Geneva Conventions (contrary to a Supreme Court ruling) and exempts government agents from the criminal penalties of the War Crimes Act. The results are the same: U.S. government officials cannot be charged with war crimes for the use of torturous interrogation techniques in the war on terror.

Perhaps in this unconventional war against an ambiguous enemy, a new strategy is necessary to make it look as though so many of our sons, daughters, husbands, wives, brothers, sisters, neighbors, cousins, and friends are dying for a reason. For argument's sake, assume for a moment that there is more to this war than power and oil and vengeance, and that the actual goal the Bush Administration is working so diligently to achieve is to prevent future terrorism. It is possible that the Administration had our best interests in mind when it hatched this "immune from Geneva Conventions" plan. But using torture to extend democratic freedoms and prevent terrorism is not only insanely hypocritical; it's illegal, it appeals to our lowest instincts, *and it doesn't work.*

The use of torture is proscribed by not only the Geneva Conventions and the federal War Crimes Act of 1996, but also by the Eighth Amendment to the Constitution ("Excessive bail shall not be required, nor excessive fines imposed, nor cruel and unusual punishments inflicted"), the constitutions and laws of every state in the Union, the UN Convention Against Torture, the Universal Declaration of Human Rights, the Uniform Code of Military Justice, the Detainee Treatment Act of 2005, and the International Covenant on Civil and Political Rights. But beyond the searing criminality of torture, the reality is that if the torturer needs the truth, torture simply doesn't work.

According to Army Col. Stuart Herrington, a military intelligence specialist assigned by the Pentagon to assess interrogations in Iraq, six out of ten prisoners can be persuaded to talk without the use of any "stress measures" at all, let alone cruel and humiliating ones. In fact, many of those involved in terrorist activities are so proud of their actions and what they stand for that they will freely acknowledge them as a perverse badge of honor. The remaining four, under the duress of torture, will tell the interrogator whatever they think the interrogator wants to hear, even if that means fabricating the stories entirely.[6]

"You can get anyone to confess to anything if the torture's bad enough," former CIA officer Robert Baer told ABC's Brian Ross. For two weeks, Ibn al-Shaykh al-Libbi, a paramilitary trainer for al-Qaeda, was subjected to progressively aggressive interrogation techniques by American and Egyptian forces. Finally, after being waterboarded (discussion to follow) and then left to stand naked in a cell overnight where he was doused repeatedly with ice-cold water, al-Libbi told the interrogators what they wanted to hear: Iraq had trained al-Qaeda members to use biochemical weapons. His statements were used by President Bush as evidence of a connection between Saddam Hussein and al-Qaeda to justify invading Iraq. It was later established that al-Libbi fabricated the confession because he was terrified of further torture.[7] But President Bush relied on what he said and represented it as the truth to the American people.

Despite the fact that the credibility of information culled from torture is questionable at best, a January 2007 investigation by the FBI into allegations of abuse of the Gitmo detainees revealed that cruel and inhumane interrogation practices continue. The report revealed that Gitmo guards bragged about beating the detainees and described it as common practice. It also documents more than two dozen incidents of abuse and mistreatment, including prisoners chained in fetal positions on the floor or hung by their hands from the ceiling; prolonged exposure to extremes of temperature, loud music, and flashing lights; electrical shocks; deprivation of food and water; and the controversial simulated drowning process known as "waterboarding."[8]

The report also included accounts of severe psychological torture, including a variety of techniques aimed at sexually humiliating prisoners and desecrating their religious beliefs. One such account reported that a female guard handled the genitals of and wiped menstrual blood on the faces of detainees. Another military interrogator reportedly bragged to an FBI agent about dressing as a Catholic priest, "baptizing" a prisoner, and throwing his Qur'an into a toilet.[9] This is your government at work.

OUTSOURCING TORTURE

The man suddenly became aware of the changing cabin pressure. He was blindfolded, then chained to the floor of the airplane. Through the groggy haze the man began to remember a bus ride. A police station. Eight masked figures looming over him. He remembered being bound and his eyes covered. His clothes had been cut off. He flinched at the recollection of an enema and a diaper. Then the burning sensation of an injection into his arm, and then blackness. He didn't know how much time had passed, who the masked figures were, or where they were taking him.

He heard the tires squeal against the runway. He was taken to a cold, dirty cell. He was kicked and beaten and warned by an interrogator, "You are here in a country where no one knows about you, in a country where there is no law. If you die, we will bury you, and no one will ever know." The interrogator spoke American-accented English.[10]

Khalid el-Masri, a German citizen of Arab descent, was imprisoned in the "Salt Pit," a secret CIA prison in Afghanistan. For five months el-Masri was kept in solitary confinement, beaten, and relentlessly interrogated. The only "evidence" against him was that his name *resembled* that of someone *believed* to be a *friend* of a September 11th hijacker. In spite of the underwhelming evidence against him, the director of the CIA's al-Qaeda unit ordered el-Masri captured and extradited to the American-run prison in Afghanistan.

It didn't take long for the CIA to confirm that el-Masri's passport was valid and that he was not the man they were looking for. Five months after his abduction, he was deposited on a narrow country road in Albania at dusk. As he walked from the vehicle, he felt very certain he was about to be shot in the back.

Khalid el-Masri was one of innumerable victims of extraordinary rendition. This top secret practice of abducting terror suspects and transferring them into the control of foreign governments or to one of the CIA's "black sites," so that interrogation methods that do not comply with U.S. laws may be applied to the suspects, has become increasingly useful as the legal support for the extrajudicial military tribunal system at Gitmo crumbles.

The extraordinary rendition policy is not an invention of the Bush Administration. Its roots trace back to the Reagan era. In those days, drug traffickers and terrorism suspects would be captured and brought into the United States, where they were given lawyers and put on trial. After the 1993 World Trade Center attack, the policy shifted to allow suspected Islamic terrorists to be taken to a third country in order to avoid U.S. laws prescribing due process and proscribing torture.

The United Nations Convention Against Torture (to which the United States is a signatory) proscribes the transfer of prisoners into the custody of a country where there are "substantial grounds" for believing they will be tortured. But, unsurprisingly, the White House has managed to manipulate the language and claim it doesn't apply to extraordinary renditions, arguing that they could not be sure whether suspects would be tortured or not.[11] President Bill Clinton granted the CIA permission to use rendition in a 1995 presidential directive.[12]

But since the start of the war on terror, the Bush Administration has dramatically expanded the use of this clandestine program. Hundreds of people suspected of being terrorists, or of providing support or intelligence to terrorist organizations, have been transported to other countries, such as Egypt, Afghanistan, Jordan, Iraq, Syria, and Uzbekistan, and to black sites throughout Eastern Europe.

An investigation by a committee of the European Parliament found more than twelve hundred CIA-operated flights had utilized European airports on their way to secret detention centers between 2001 and 2005.[13] And even as the European media roars over revelations that Poland and Romania housed secret CIA prisons, the Bush Administration continued to deny the existence of the black sites and the illegal extraordinary rendition process.

> **Contrary to what your government wants you to believe, what happened at Abu Ghraib was not an isolated incident.**

But contrary to what your government wants you to believe, what happened at Abu Ghraib was not an isolated incident. It was not the result of a few rotten apples. It was the tip of a much larger and more disturbing iceburg.

According to former CIA agent Robert Baer, whom I have met personally and interviewed many times on Fox News Radio, "If you want a serious interrogation, you send a prisoner to Jordan. If you want them to be tortured, you send them to Syria. If you want someone to disappear, never to see them again, you send them to Egypt."[14]

A 2005 report on renditions compiled by the Center for Human Rights and Global Justice at New York University School of Law documented accounts of several victims who have all come forward with similar tales of abduction, beatings, blindfolds, shackles, and months of torture and interrogations. The exact number of people who have been kidnapped and taken to the secret prisons is unknown since (unsurprisingly) all information regarding operations is classified as, no surprise here, state secrets.

"VE HAF VAYS OF MAKING YOU TALK!"

In 2002, Maher Arar, a Syrian-born Canadian citizen, was detained at John F. Kennedy International Airport in New York City. He was held for thirteen days and interrogated about his connection to a terrorism suspect, the brother of a work colleague, without access to lawyers. Instead of being extradited to Canada, his country of citizenship where he has lived lawfully for the past nineteen years, he was shackled by your government and put on board a small private jet.

Arar was taken to Syria, where he was thrown into a small, three-by-six-foot, underground cell that was unlit and infested with rats. He was ruthlessly beaten with shredded cables and forced to confess that he had attended an al-Qaeda training camp in Afghanistan. "I was willing to do anything to stop the torture," he said.[15] Through the walls of his cell, Mr. Arar could hear the screams of other prisoners who were also being tortured.

He was held for ten months. Under pressure from Mr. Arar's wife, the Canadian government eventually took up his case, and he was returned to Canada. No terrorist links were ever found. No apology was ever given. No compensation was ever offered.

WHAT'S IN A WORD?

In 2003, Laid Saidi was seized in Tanzania with a fake passport. He was turned over to CIA agents and flown to Afghanistan and chained to a wall in the "salt pit," in a cell that neighbored Mr. el-Masri's. He was suspended from the ceiling by his hands and interrogated daily about a telephone conversation about airplanes. When the tape was finally played for Mr. Saidi, he realized that whoever had been monitoring the conversation had interpreted the discussion to be about airplanes (*tayarat* in Arabic), when he was actually talking about selling tires (*tirat* in Arabic). Mr. Saidi was held for sixteen months before being returned to his native Algeria without charge.[16]

Considering that there are no congressionally approved guidelines, no judicial review processes, no accountability or requirements of any showing of proof, it is impossible to know how many persons have been erroneously abducted and detained in gravelike cells at secret prisons in horrific conditions around the world at the request of your government. What's more alarming, it's also impossible to know if the use is limited to terrorism suspects.

THE CIA AND EXTRAORDINARY RENDITION

In June 2007, six leading human rights organizations compiled a report that names thirty-nine people believed to have been held in secret U.S. detention centers, whose current whereabouts remain publicly unknown.[17] They are called "disappeared" detainees. The government has refused to release any information about the location of the prisoners or their identities.

But there are Americans outside of the government who do know where they are, Americans whose Hamptons summer homes and country club memberships are made possible by the extraordinary rendition program.

The staff at Jeppesen International Trip Planning, a subsidiary of Boeing, the world's largest aerospace company and a publicly traded American corporation, arranges everything needed for "efficient, hassle-free, international flight operations."[18] Their biggest client: the CIA.

"We do all of the extraordinary rendition flights; you know, the torture flights. Let's face it, some of these flights end up that way," Jeppesen managing director Bob Overby told his employees at a staff meeting.[19]

Most of the planes used in the transportation of prisoners are owned by no-name charter airlines that are actually CIA front companies. Jeppesen handles the rest. Two of Jeppesen's trip planners are specifically assigned to handle the logistics for the rendition flights. From flight plans and air-space clearance to hotel reservations at luxury resorts for the aircraft crew, Jeppesen knows how to

> "We do all of the extraordinary rendition flights; you know, the torture flights. Let's face it, some of these flights end up that way."
>
> —Jeppesen managing director Bob Overby

keep its clients happy. And, according to Bob Overby, the CIA makes complicity for kidnapping and torture worth their while.

"It certainly pays well. [The CIA] spare[s] no expense. They have absolutely no worry about costs. What they have to get done, they get done," said Overby.[20]

Private corporations should not be profiting from this illegal torture program. Worse, our government should not be using your tax dollars to pay private corporations to break the law!

But the American public barely flinched when the story of Mr. el-Masri broke. The price of Boeing stock held steady. Mr. el-Masri filed suit against CIA Director George Tenet and several CIA employees in an attempt to obtain justice for his illegal abduction and torture. United States District Court Judge T. S. Ellis agreed with government arguments that moving forward with the case would risk national security by exposing, no surprise, state secrets about CIA activities vital to the U.S. war on terrorism, and he dismissed the case.

"While dismissal of the complaint deprives el-Masri of an American judicial forum for vindicating his claims . . . el-Masri's private interests must give way to the national interest in preserving state secrets," Judge Ellis wrote in his opinion.[21]

If private interests as grave as being abducted, taken to a remote area of the world, thrown in a dungeon, and tortured for months on end are subordinate to the government's ability to operate outside the law and torture prisoners without the constraints of the legal system or public opinion, then the national interest is a serious threat to the rest of our basic civil liberties.

The word *terror* still invokes a wave of fear in the sheep, and they want to believe that the government is trying to protect them, that torture is a last resort, and the only way to prevent future terrorism. But the wolves know better. The wolves know that it's only a matter of time until the war on terror shifts and a new incarnation of terrorist will be the target of these renditions. Is there an end to the government's choices or torture targets?

14

THE DYING BREATHS OF
THE FREE PRESS

The press in a democratic society is often equated to the "fourth branch" of government; a watchdog charged with keeping the government accountable to the people. When a government wants more power over the population, the press is historically among the first to go. Democracy depends on an informed electorate; where the free press dies, democracy soon follows. Our Founding Fathers recognized that an independent media is the linchpin that allows a democratic society to function, and in the very first amendment to the Constitution, they protected the press from government interference.

But like so many of the other foundational liberties, freedom of the press has been a target of the government's assault on the Constitution. Although the government does not have the power to censor the press directly, it has mastered the art of manipulating the members of the mainstream media into censoring themselves.

In the post-September 11th world, members of the U.S. news media have become sheep; passive platforms for the government's version of events. Whether it is pressure for sales or ratings, intimidation by the Administration, or a fear of looking unpatriotic, virtually all of the leading news outlets have censored their coverage of the war on terror and the policy of the Bush Administration.

After former Attorney General John Ashcroft essentially charged any journalist who was critical of the Administration or who reported disturbing, unflattering truths about the war as supporters of terrorism,[1] objectivity dissolved and the news media fell quickly in line.

In the lead-up to the war, the Pentagon developed a sweeping plan to control press coverage of combat. The rules were designed to ensure that a sanitized picture of the war was sent home to the public. The government handpicked and assigned five hundred reporters to be "embedded" within military units. Journalists were not permitted to use their own transportation, limiting access to only what military command wanted them to see. Unit commanders had control over all dispatches. If journalists came in contact with sensitive information, they were warned that it would be inappropriate to report on it.

Instead of lambasting this military orchestration of press coverage, reporters, photographers, and news crews volunteered for the propaganda corps and went off to war-reporter boot camp to prepare for deployment.

Back in the newsroom, television and newspaper editorial staffs were instructed to counter reports of war casualties with references to World Trade Center deaths and refrain from printing images of dead Iraqi and Afghan civilians for fear of appearing unpatriotic. Even *CBS Evening News* anchor Dan Rather, no friend of George W. Bush, pledged his allegiance to the war effort when he told *Late Night* host David Letterman: "Wherever [the president] wants me to line up, just tell me where. And he'll make the call."[2] No wonder he lost his job.

TELLING THE TRUTH IS TREASON

But an intrepid few refuse to follow the flock. From the *New York Times* exposé of the NSA's warrantless eavesdropping and data mining programs, to ABC's reporting of the secret CIA prisons and the covert U.S. operations in Iran to destabilize the government, some members of the press have fought to cover stories that the federal government works overtime to keep out of the headlines. *USA Today*, for instance, uncovered the government's collection of phone records from the major carriers, including AT&T, Verizon, and BellSouth (but not Qwest, which refused, like a wolf, to cooperate in a scheme its general counsel no doubt advised was illegal).

Brian Ross, a prominent investigative reporter at ABC and from time to time a guest on my radio show, recently exposed the fact that President Bush directed the CIA to carry out secret operations against Iran, including the placement of negative newspaper articles, propaganda broadcasts, and the manipulation of Iran's currency and international banking transactions.[3] A GOP presidential hopeful, former Massachusetts Governor Mitt Romney, quickly came out swinging against ABC and Ross for potentially endangering American lives and jeopardizing national security.[4]

It is no coincidence that Brian Ross's excellent reporting also landed him on the government's short list of people to monitor. Ross and another ABC colleague were warned by a source, "It's time for you to get some new cell phones, quick."[5] In an interview with PBS, Ross even stated that one of his law enforcement sources told his colleague, "We know who you're calling. I know who you called. You've got to be careful here; they're tracking you." Since Ross is being monitored by government wiretaps, he has been forced to conduct many more face-to-face interviews and far fewer interviews over the phone.

IF IT'S NOT TREASON, IT'S ESPIONAGE!

The Espionage Act of 1917 made it a crime to oppose war publicly and openly. The Act states that "when the United States is at war" anyone who shall "willfully utter, print, write or publish any disloyal, profane, scurrilous, or abusive language about the form of government of the United States . . . (the war, the flag, the military, the navy, enlistments, buying bonds, uniforms, etc.)" faces the possibility of being charged with espionage.[6]

Although antiquated and wildly unconstitutional, the Espionage Act has never officially been rescinded, and the Bush Administration has at least considered its viability as a tool to control the free press.

After the *New York Times* exposed that President Bush had authorized the illegal NSA eavesdropping program, Attorney General Alberto Gonzales seemed to be suggesting the use of the Espionage Act against the *Times*. On ABC's *This Week* in May 2006, Gonzales was asked, "So you believe journalists can be prosecuted for publishing classified information?" He replied, "There are some statutes on the book[s] which, if you read the language carefully, would seem to indicate that that is a possibility . . . we have an obligation to ensure that our national security is protected."[7] After the article was published, many conservative blogs railed against the *New York Times*, calling it the "Paper of Treason." What these legions of sheep overlook is that without the press to inform us of our government's covert attacks on our civil liberties, their own ability to speak and blog freely would be seriously diminished.

PRESS TERRORISTS

Sami al-Haj was born in 1969 and raised in central Sudan. As a young boy, his brother recalled Sami's keen interest in reading, writing, and photography. Disappointed with the lack of journalism opportunities in the Sudan, Sami put his dream on hold to pursue other jobs throughout the Middle East. In the late 1990s, he met his wife, they had a child, and the family settled in Qatar. In April 2000, Sami was finally able to pursue his childhood dream of a career in journalism and accepted a job at Al Jazeera. Sami was very ambitious and eager to prove himself in order to make up for his lack of experience.

Sami's big break came after September 11th, when he volunteered to go to Afghanistan to capture exclusive images from the war zone. Equipped with a handheld camera and videophone, Sami went to Afghanistan in October 2001 and spent two months putting in fifteen-hour days, capturing images of civilian fallout from U.S. bombs. At the time, the images and footage that Sami secured were some of the only information coming out of southeastern Afghanistan.

On December 15th 2001, Sami's dreams of a successful career in journalism were put on hold when he was crossing into Afghanistan from Pakistan's Chaman crossing point. Sami was detained at the crossing, which was quite confusing to him, considering that he just traveled across a different border crossing a few days earlier. Upon questioning, the border guard produced Sami's old Sudanese passport number (which he lost years earlier), but when a Pakistani intelligence official arrived, Sami was told not to worry. The next day the intelligence official took Sami away in a car. It was the last time Sami was seen as a free man.

Sami was routed through several countries before he ended up in Cuba at Gitmo in June 2002. Sami is the only known journalist imprisoned at Gitmo. Sami has not been charged with a crime, and all of the evidence against him, if there actually is any, is, you guessed it, a state secret. Therefore neither Sami nor his lawyer even knows what "evidence" the United States government believes links Sami to a crime. All they know is that the U.S. seems to be more interested in Sami's work with Al Jazeera, its staff, and their satellite activity than with his alleged ties to terrorism.

Sami has fulfilled his childhood dream of getting published, but unfortunately it isn't because he wrote the story on the front page of the *New York Times*. Instead some of Sami's poetry has been published in an eighty-four-page anthology titled *Poems from Guantánamo: The Detainees Speak* which he wrote while confined at Gitmo in his eight-by-seven-foot cell wondering why he is there.

THE "FREE" PRESS?

But Sami is not the only journalist currently being held by U.S. forces. Bilal Hussein, a photographer for the Associated Press, has been imprisoned by the U.S. military since April 2006. Bilal was on assignment covering the war in Iraq when he was arrested by U.S. forces for "imperative reasons of security." Hussein is a Pulitzer Prize–winning photographer for the Associated Press.

Executive editor and senior vice president of the AP, Kathleen Carroll, said that Bilal Hussein has not even been questioned since May 2006, and the AP believes that he is being held because of his photographs from within the Anbar province. Hussein has yet to be charged with any criminal activity, and the military has not disclosed any evidence to demonstrate a reason for Hussein's imprisonment.

Mr. Hussein is just one of dozens of Iraqi journalists to be captured and held without charges by the United States.[8]

NOT YOURSPACE!

Even though the Bush Administration has largely won its campaign against independence and objectivity in the mainstream media, the Internet has created a new set of challenges. For one, it has radically fueled the "information revolution" and may be truly the last bastion of the free "press." Never before have so many people had access to sources of news and opinions from around the world. With the increased popularity of blogging and video-sharing sites such as YouTube, anyone, anywhere, who has access to a camera and a computer, can be a reporter.

Now, soldiers serve as frontline reporters, with helmet-mounted cameras and digital photos of carnage from Iraq and elsewhere. They are quickly becoming an integral component in the news-gathering machine, offering us candid and uncensored coverage of battles and skirmishes that are highly editorialized in the mainstream media.

Until now.

Your government does not look favorably on footage of the war in Iraq, such as the collection of videos compiled under the title "Iraq Uploaded" on MTV's Web site.[9] The videos are a homemade portrait of day-to-day moments in the war, and their raw, compelling presentation separates them from footage seen in mainstream media. Since the publication of "Iraq Uploaded" in July 2006, the military has banned the use of mtv.com, among other Web sites, on the computers used by your soldiers in Iraq. The government also censors the messages that soldiers post on the Internet, manipulating the impression of the war formed by those on the homefront.

> **The government also censors the messages that soldiers post on the Internet, manipulating the impression of the war formed by those on the homefront.**

Under Army Regulation 530–1: Operations Security (OPSEC), before your troops can post a Web log (blog), post a comment to an Internet message board, or even send an e-mail home to their families, they must get their immediate superior's approval. Failure to do so could result in court-martial or administrative, disciplinary, contractual, or criminal actions.

However, Major Ray Ceralde said there is some leeway in the rules, because "it is not practical to check all communication, especially private communication." Some units might only require the initial blog registration, whereas "other units may require a review before every posting."[10]

Jeff Nuding, who won the Bronze Star for his service in Iraq, speculates that "many commanders will feel like they have no choice but to forbid their soldiers from blogging—or even using email. If I'm a commander, and think that any slip-up gets me screwed, I'm making it easy: No blogs!"[11]

The army has even gone so far as to activate a team, the Army Web Risk Assessment Cell, to scan blogs for information breaches. An official army dispatch told military bloggers, "Big Brother is not watching you, but 10 members of a Virginia National Guard unit might be."[12]

Active-duty troops are not the only ones affected by these new regulations, because the broad language also includes civilians working for the military, army contractors, and even soldiers' families.

Passing on classified data has long been a serious crime. But the new regulations take an extremely expansive view of what unclassified information the enemy could potentially find useful.

On May 14th 2007, the Defense Department began blocking Web sites such as YouTube, MySpace, Live365, and BlackPlanet, to name a few.[13] In all, thirteen of the most popular social networking Web sites have been banned on military computers—sites that could have allowed soldiers to keep in touch with family and friends via messages, pictures, and audio/video recordings.

> An official army dispatch told military bloggers, "Big Brother is not watching you, but 10 members of a Virginia National Guard unit might be."

The government said the ban was a response to concern that increased use of these sites would overwhelm the military's private Internet network and risk disclosure of combat-sensitive material. Do you accept that? These sites offer an invaluable connection to the real world for the men and women of the United States Armed Forces. They are places to quell homesickness and connect with faraway friends and family; chances for a laugh at the end of an emotionally brutal day; uncensored opportunities to express the hardship, frustration, fear, anger, and hope that come along with being a soldier.

Mitchell Millican of Trafford, Alabama, relied on MySpace in order to keep in touch with his son, Pfc. Jonathan M. Millican, before he was killed on January 20th 2007. Jonathan's freedom to use MySpace allowed Mitchell to talk with his son just three days before he died.[14] Now, no soldier is afforded that freedom, not from a military computer. The troops are allowed to use *private* computers to go to these restricted Web sites. But very few soldiers actually carry private computers while in combat zones, and there are few Internet cafes in Afghanistan and Iraq.

The new rules on military blogs, or "milblogs," are still being felt out due to differing opinions on how they will actually affect the troops. Army OPSEC Program Manager Major Ray Ceralde said that the new policy would have no effect on blogging. Blogger John Donovan said, however, that he is worried that "commanders might interpret the new policy to mean that they have to read every blog post before it goes on line," which could create a bottleneck for the commanders, to the point where they simply forbid blogging entirely.[15]

Censoring these sites is a violation of one of the essential liberties your military risks their lives for, while defending our country and the very Constitution that guarantees the right to free speech. It is a selfish attempt to maintain domestic support for the war on terror by shaping the image of war shown in the media. Meanwhile, the government is effectively secluding the men and women fighting for their country from the people they're fighting for and robbing them of their First Amendment protected right to freedom of speech.

15

WHERE DO WE GO
FROM HERE?

In planning and writing this book, I was not sure where to stop recounting the parade of horribles that the American government has visited upon us. It seems that almost every day someone in the executive branch of the federal government is caught either violating federal law with the president's blessings in the name of safety, or announcing that the president needs more unconstitutional powers to keep us safe. As I write this, Congress has just voted, after very little debate in the House and Senate, to change the Foreign Intelligence Surveillance Act (FISA) so as to purport to give the president the legal authority to spy on Americans by listening to our telephone conversations and monitoring our computer keystrokes when we communicate with persons outside the United States, without a warrant issued by a judge. The president told Congress that the situation was grave and debate unnecessary. I wrote above "purport to give" because Congress lacks the authority to enable the president to spy on Americans without a search warrant. The Constitution prohibits such behavior, and Congress cannot change the Constitution. Period.

Also as I write this, three horrific, execution-style murders in my birthplace, Newark, New Jersey, have captivated the nation. Unfortunately, they have animated the local county sheriff who told a newspaper reporter: "I'm on the verge of telling my guys to suspend civil liberties, and start frisking everybody."[1] This is a sheriff obviously unfit for office. He cannot suspend the rights that are natural to us and guaranteed by the Constitution; but he is dangerous to freedom because he thinks he can.

Why should government agents spy on us? They work for *us*. How about we spy on them? On cops when they arrest and interrogate people or contemplate suspending freedom; on prosecutors when they decide who to prosecute and what evidence to use; on judges when they rationalize away our guaranteed rights; and on members of Congress whenever they meet with a lobbyist, mark up a piece of legislation, or conspire to assault our liberties or our pocketbooks? These are all *our* employees, and *we* have the right to know what *they* are doing.

Apparently, most members of Congress and at least one New Jersey sheriff do not take seriously their oaths to uphold the Supreme Law of the Land, as the Constitution declares itself to be. Congress votes casually and regularly, and often without reading the proposed legislation on which it is voting, to remove or diminish rights guaranteed by the Constitution. The new FISA law just adds to the long litany of government lawlessness laid out in this book. And the New Jersey sheriff's public threat to suspend freedom is breathtaking in its malignity.

It is beyond comprehension for the Congress and the president and any judges or sheriffs to assault any part of the Constitution. They are sworn to uphold all of it. Much of the Constitution comes from our English forebears, but the Fourth Amendment is uniquely American. It has been the victim of most of the government's lawless behavior. The Fourth Amendment establishes the truly American value of privacy. Justice Brandeis called privacy "the most comprehensive of rights and the right most valued by civilized men," namely "the right to be le[f]t alone."[2] The Fourth Amendment was written because the Founders were sick and tired of British soldiers writing their own search warrants as a pretext for coming onto and into the colonists' property, even when there was no demonstrable evidence of criminal activity on the part of the person whose property was being searched.

The Fourth Amendment puts a neutral judge between the government and its target; no matter how evil the target, no matter how dangerous the target, no matter how widespread the belief of the target's guilt, no matter how accurate the belief in the target's guilt, and no matter who the target is or what he knows. The Constitution requires the government to demonstrate probable cause of a crime before a judge can authorize unleashing the government's use of force on the target. We have, sadly, given the government a monopoly on the use of force. The Fourth Amendment regulates that monopoly.

> The Fourth Amendment was written because the Founders were sick and tired of British soldiers writing their own search warrants as a pretext for coming onto and into the colonists' property.

It is Fourth Amendment protections that have saved us and all past generations of Americans from the knock on the door in the middle of the night, from Grandpa and Junior disappearing forever with government agents like in the banana republics, and from unwanted soldiers or agents looking for whatever they want to take for themselves.

What is it about Congresspersons, high-ranking government

officials, judges, sheriffs, even presidents, that induces or allows them to think that they can write any statute, enforce any policy, break any law, or disregard any constitutional guarantee without regard to the Constitution they have sworn to uphold? Are they in utter ignorance of the preexisting laws they were elected to enforce or appointed to safeguard? Do they not realize that they are in violation of the natural law that governs us all? I have thought long and hard about this, because disregard for the Constitution and for natural law among those in government is so rampant, frequent, and troublesome. It must be, as Lord Acton famously stated, that "power corrupts, and absolute power corrupts absolutely." The corruption of which he wrote was not in the sense of bribery, but of acquiring power for the wrong purpose: Not to liberate or to preserve freedom, but for the internal personal gratification that its exercise affords; and acquiring so much power that one sees oneself as the master, and no longer as the public servant.

The whole purpose of the Constitution is to limit, separate, diffuse, and check the use of power. The Founders insisted on this because of their experience both with British monarchs, whose power over individuals was virtually unchecked, and with British Parliaments, which could (and still can) write any law regulating any aspect of human behavior without regard to a written constitution (the British have none) and without regard to the natural law. They knew that an enforceable constitution that guaranteed natural rights, that specifically delineated who had the power to do what, and that expressly forbade the government from interfering with the exercise of natural rights would be the best instrument for preserving human freedom.

They were right.

But, with the passage of time, with government assaults on liberty during wartime accepted by sheep-like Americans, and with a wink and a nod, government lawbreaking has become the rule, fear the means, power the end, and liberty the victim in the everyday operation of government in America today.

There is little we can do about this but warn our fellow Americans of liberty lost. At this writing, sixteen politicians are competing nationally to replace President Bush; there are eight Democrats and eight Republicans. With the exception of Rep. Ron Paul (R-TX), in terms of fidelity to the Constitution, it does not matter which one of them wins. Except for Congressman Paul, they all love power for its own sake, believe that Big Government should redistribute wealth, regard the Constitution as a quaint obstacle, and would enforce or disregard laws as they saw fit; all this, without regard to our history, our values, or our natural rights.

> With the passage of time, with government assaults on liberty during wartime accepted by sheep-like Americans, and with a wink and a nod, government lawbreaking has become the rule, fear the means, power the end, and liberty the victim in the everyday operation of government in America today.

Term limits might help weed out those whose goal in government is permanent control over others, as their tenure would be brief. Abolition of the Sixteenth Amendment would deny the federal government the right to tax our incomes and would force it to live within more reasonable means, and have less money to use to tamper with our liberties. Abolishing the Seventeenth Amendment would return the election of senators to state legislatures, thus assuring that the Congress respected the limits on its powers. Expelling from Congress all members who vote for legislation subsequently found unconstitutional and requiring every member of Congress to identify and certify under oath the specific grant of power in the Constitution that forms the basis for each vote taken on each piece of legislation would keep their hands off our freedoms.

But the problem with government in America today is that it attracts primarily those who want to expand it. If men and women were angels, as James Madison once hoped, or if all—even most—members of Congress were truly faithful to the Constitution, the evils this book has related would go away. Don't hold your breath. Jefferson understood all of this when he lamented that "the natural progress of things is for liberty to yield and government to gain ground."

> The problem with government in America today is that it attracts primarily those who want to expand it.

And it could get a lot worse. A friend who spent his career in the CIA tells me that there is almost no end to the lengths to which the powers of darkness will go to make us the nation of the watched, notwithstanding the Fourth Amendment. Government scientists, I have been told, can now turn on your cell phone remotely, while it is in your pocket or purse, and monitor and record whatever they hear. Of course, if done without a search warrant issued by a judge, that is a criminal act. The current vice president is known to favor the mandatory implantation of computer chips into the necks or arms of those whose behavior the government wishes to monitor most closely. Where is that power in the Constitution? That, too, is far beyond the lawful ability of Congress to authorize. The former happened without our knowing it because we are sheep. The latter would, I hope, bring out the wolf in all of us. If the government can implant computer chips in those it wishes to monitor, it can implant them in anyone. Your pet would have more freedom than you. What to make of a government that would treat us as dogs? It will be time to vote to "alter or abolish" any government that would do such things, as the Declaration of Independence demands.

. America desperately needs a reawakening to freedom. We need men and women who will dedicate themselves to defending the rights of individuals as defined by the natural law and guaranteed by the Constitution; and we need them in government.

We need ordinary folks to stop acting like sheep: Monitor your elected officials; make them account for all of their votes; recall or impeach them when they tamper with freedom. Write and blog about all they do.

> **If the government can implant computer chips in those it wishes to monitor, it can implant them in anyone. Your pet would have more freedom than you. What to make of a government that would treat us as dogs? It will be time to vote to "alter or abolish" any government that would do such things, as the Declaration of Independence demands.**

And reject profoundly the satanic bargain which the sheep have accepted that less freedom equals more safety.

Less freedom equals slavery.

If we surrender our freedoms in order to defend the nation, what would be left that is worth defending?

ACKNOWLEDGMENTS

I have many colleagues and friends whose work, patience, and understanding have contributed in large measure to this book. My friend James C. Sheil, a gifted lawyer, writer, and editor, has spent many hours using his skills to tighten my language and better illuminate my ideas. My research assistants, Rachel DeLetto, Donald D'Amico, and Alyson Mansfield, all worked tirelessly and with great passion, and their work was invaluable to me. My radio partner, Brian Kilmeade, who challenges many of my ideas, is a daily sounding board. My friend Andy Muldoon, a brilliant economist, has spent countless hours with me, analyzing the evils of unconstitutional government. My friend, classmate, and godson, Thomas Harding Jones, who died during the final work on this book, inspired many of my attitudes about minimal government and maximum individual liberties. He believed, as do I, that our rights are natural gifts from God, an integral part of our humanity, and cannot be legislated or given or ordered away. My personal assistant at Fox, Tamara Gitt, and my personal producer at Fox, Kathryn Klein, have happily endured all the stress their boss can convey when writing a book. And my boss at Fox, Roger Ailes, one of the great media personalities of our day, has generously given me all the opportunities I have sought in television, radio, and publishing. Without his great brain and big heart, you would not know of me or this book.

NOTES

INTRODUCTION

1. http://www.whitehouse.gov/news/releases/2002/11/20021112-1.html.
2. This phrase was used in a letter from the Pennsylvania Assembly, dated November 11th 1755, to the governor of Pennsylvania. It also appears in an epigraph on the title page of *An Historical Review of the Constitution and Government of Pennsylvania,* an anonymous book published in 1759. Both the quote and the book were originally attributed to Benjamin Franklin but were later attributed to Richard Jackson.

CHAPTER 1

1. 12 Harv. J.L. & Pub. Policy 63 (1989).
2. *U.S. v. Robel,* 389 U.S. 258 (1967).
3. Richard Jackson, *An Historical Review of the Constitution and Government of Pennsylvania,* 289. (This quote was first attributed to Benjamin Franklin.)
4. Martin Luther King Jr., "Letter from Birmingham Jail."
5. John Locke, *Second Treatise on Government,* Ch. II, sec. VI.
6. Thomas Paine, *The Rights of Man,* Elibron Classic edition (1791; Adamant Media Corporation, 2006), front matter. Citations are to the Elibron edition.
7. Declaration of Independence.
8. George W. Bush, Inaugural Address, 2005.

CHAPTER 2

1. *Whitney v. California,* 274 U.S. 357 @ 375–376.
2. Project Safe *and* Free, http://www.aclu.org/safefree/general/20131prs200 50810.html.
3. "NYCLU Sues New York City over Subway Bag Search Policy," August 4th 2005, http://www.aclu.org/police/searchseizure/20054prs20050804.html.
4. *MacWade v. Kelly,* 460 F 3d 260 (2006).
5. "Finger Scanning at Disney Parks Causes Concern," http://www.local6 .com/news/4724689/detail.html.
6. Jim Dwyer, "City Police Spied Broadly Before G.O.P. Convention," *New York Times,* March 25th 2007, http://www.psfp.com/nytimes_surveillance/ny pdspiedbroadly.htm.

7. Ibid.
8. Ibid.
9. *Lederman v. Giuliani,* S.D.N.Y., 2001; ibid.
10. Jim Dwyer, "Judge Says Police Violated Rules in Videotaping Public Gatherings," *New York Times,* Feburary 16th 2007, http://graphics.nytimes.com/packages/pdf/nyregion/20070215_nycruling.pdf.

CHAPTER 3

1. See the Sedition Act of 1798, sec. 2.
2. Michael Kent Curtis, "Free Speech, the People's Darling Privilege." (Durham: Duke University Press, 2000. Michael Kent Curtis offers an excellent and detailed account of the troubled affair between Clement Vallandigham and Abraham Lincoln in this work.
3. *Darke County Democrat* May 5th 1863.
4. Judge Leavitt in Vallandigham Habeas Corpus case 1863, http://www.daytonhistorybooks.citymax.com/page/page/1698215.htm.
5. Harry Ketcham, *The Life of Abraham Lincoln,* ch. 40, http://www.authorama.com/life-of-abraham-lincoln-42.html.
6. Wikipedia, s.v. "Vallandigham."
7. Horatio Seymour, in Henry J. Raymond, *The Life and Public Services of Abraham Lincoln, Sixteenth President of The United States; Together with His State Papers, Including His Speeches, Addresses, Messages, Letters, and Proclamations, and the Closing Scenes Connected with His Life and Death* (Derby and Miller, 1865), 368. PDF available from http://books.google.com.
8. "Gov. Seymour's Letter," *New York Times,* May 19th 1863, 4 (available in *New York Times* archives).
9. Abraham Lincoln, "Letter to Erastus Corning and Others," June 12th 1863, http://www.teachingamericanhistory.org/library/index.asp?documentprint=612.
10. John G. Nicolay and John Hay, eds., *Abraham Lincoln: Complete Works, Comprising His Speeches, Letters, State Papers and Miscellaneous Writings,* vol. 2 (The Century Co., 1894).
11. *Wimmer v. U.S.,* 264 Fed. 11, at 12.
12. The *Wimmer* case is fairly obscure, but much of the relevant information is available in the court's decision itself, available at 264 F. 11.
13. Merriam-Webster Online, http://www.m-w.com/dictionary/anarchism, accessed August 17th 2007.
14. Wyatt Kingseed, "President William McKinley: Assassinated by an Anarchist," HistoryNet.com, http://www.historynet.com/ah/blassassinationmckinley/.
15. Ibid.
16. N.Y. Penal Law §§160-161 (repealed 1967).
17. "McKinley Assassination Ink," sec. 1, § 468-a, http://mckinleydeath.com/documents/govdocs/LSNY1902.htm.
18. Ibid.

19. Todd J. Pfannestiel, *Rethinking the Red Scare* (New York: Routledge, 2003), 22.
20. "Larkin and Gitlow Held in $15,000," *New York Times* Archives, November 11th 1919, 1.
21. *Gitlow v. People of New York*, No. 19 Supreme Court of The United States 268 U.S. 652; 45 S. Ct. 625; 1925 U.S., June 8th 1925, http://www.hrcr.org /safrica/expression/gitlow_ny.html.
22. Wikipedia, s.v., "*Gitlow v. New York*, 268 U.S. 652."
23. Louis Henkin and Albert J. Rosenthal, *Constitutionalism and Rights* (Columbia University Press, 1989), 85.
24. http://www.presidency.ucsb.edu/ws/index.php?pid=16068.
25. "Court Reverses Korematsu Conviction—*Korematsu v. U.S.*, 584 F.Supp. 1406, 16 Fed. R. Evid. Serv. 1231 (N.D.Cal. Apr 19th 1984)," LSU Law Center's Medical and Public Health Law Site, http://biotech.law.lsu.edu /cases/pp/korematsu_II.htm.
26. *Korematsu v. U.S.*, 323 U.S. 214 (1944) (Murphy, Dissenting).
27. Wikipedia, s.v., "Quirin."
28. Clearly Truman's integrity did not descend to the more modern administrations. In February 2005, civil rights attorney Lynne Stewart was convicted of conspiracy against the United States because of her zealous defense of accused terrorist Sheik Omar Abdel-Rahman, the leader of the Islamic group, an organization that tried to overthrow Egypt's government. For a more complete summary of the Stewart case, see Phil Hirschkorn, contrib., "Civil Rights Attorney Convicted in Terror Trial," CNN.com, February 14th 2005, http: //www.cnn.com/2005/LAW/02/10/terror.trial.lawyer/, accessed July 23rd 2007.
29. "Fair or Not, It's Legal," *Time*, April 3rd 1950, http://www.time.com/time /magazine/article/0,9171,934865,00.html?promoid=googlep.

Chapter 4

1. Program and Information Brochure on the Haymarket Tragedy of 1886, Chicago Public Library, 4–5, http://www.chipublib.org/004chicago/dis asters/text/program/4-5.html.
2. Ethan Wilensky-Lanford, "A Pretend Preacher, a Real Arrest, and a Debate About Free Speech," *New York Times*, July 1st 2007.
3. "Granny D and Author Bill McKibben Arrested in Capitol During Protest Against Campaign Corruption And Global Warming," Common Dreams Progressive Newswire, http://www.commondreams.org/news2000/0425-11 .htm. Granny D's court statement is available at http://www.grannyd.com /speeches.php?id=56&action=list.

Chapter 5

1. Nixon Tapes, 6–13, 12:18.
2. Nixon Tapes, June '71.

3. Nixon Tapes, 6-13, 12:18.
4. Nixon Tapes, wht-5-86.
5. Ibid.
6. H. R. Haldeman to President Nixon, Monday, June 14th 1971, in "The Pentagon Papers: Secrets, Lies and Audiotapes (The Nixon Tapes and the Supreme Court Tape)" National Security Archive, http://www.gwu.edu /~nsarchiv/NSAEBB/NSAEBB48/.
7. U.S. Senate, *Intelligence Activities and the Rights of Americans*: Book II (I)(2)(i) (GPO Government Printing Office, 1976).
8. Ibid., Book II (I)(3).
9. 50 USC 1802(a)(1)(A)(i).
10. 50 USC 1801 (a).
11. Ibid.
12. 50 USC 1802(a)(1)(B).
13. 50 USC 1809 & 1810.
14. For a frightening outline of the many constitutional rights that have suffered blows under the Bush tenure, see David Cole's article "The Constitution" in the June 2007 issue of *Harper's* Magazine.

CHAPTER 6

1. Naomi Wolf's brilliant editorial "Fascist America, in 10 Easy Steps," in the *Guardian* (April 24th 2007) outlines many other disturbing correlations. You can see this article at: http://www.guardian.co.uk/usa/story/0 ,,2064157,00.html.
2. David Hudson, "Patriot Act: Overview," First Amendment Center, http: //www.firstamendmentcenter.org/speech/libraries/topic.aspx?topic=patri ot_act.
3. USA Patriot Act § 213 (b)(1).
4. The full list of public accommodation facilities includes pretty much every place anyone will ever need to go:
42 USC 12181 (7) Public accommodation
The following private entities are considered public accommodations for purposes of this subchapter, if the operations of such entities affect commerce—
(A) an inn, hotel, motel, or other place of lodging, except for an establishment located within a building that contains not more than five rooms for rent or hire and that is actually occupied by the proprietor of such establishment as the residence of such proprietor;
(B) a restaurant, bar, or other establishment serving food or drink;
(C) a motion picture house, theater, concert hall, stadium, or other place of exhibition or entertainment;
(D) an auditorium, convention center, lecture hall, or other place of public gathering;
(E) a bakery, grocery store, clothing store, hardware store, shopping center, or other sales or rental establishment;

(F) a laundromat, dry-cleaner, bank, barber shop, beauty shop, travel service, shoe repair service, funeral parlor, gas station, office of an accountant or lawyer, pharmacy, insurance office, professional office of a health care provider, hospital, or other service establishment;

(G) a terminal, depot, or other station used for specified public transportation;

(H) a museum, library, gallery, or other place of public display or collection;

(I) a park, zoo, amusement park, or other place of recreation;

(J) a nursery, elementary, secondary, undergraduate, or postgraduate private school, or other place of education;

(K) a day care center, senior citizen center, homeless shelter, food bank, adoption agency, or other social service center establishment; and

(L) a gymnasium, health spa, bowling alley, golf course, or other place of exercise or recreation.

5. Nancy Chang, "The USA PATRIOT Act: What's So Patriotic About Trampling on the Bill of Rights?" November 2001, http://www.ccr-ny.org /v2/reports/docs/USA_PATRIOT_ACT.pdf.

6. 18 USCA § 2339A(b)(3).

7. http://www.firstamendmentcenter.org/speech/libraries/topic.aspx?topic =patriot_act.

8. Adam Liptak, "Sedition: It Still Rolls off the Tongue" *New York Times*, May 8th, 2006,

9. 31 USC 5312(A)(2).

10. "CRS Report for Congress," http://www.fas.org/sgp/crs/misc/98-611.pdf.

11. NSPD51/HSPD20 (2)(b) and (2)(d).

12. Passed on June 16th 1878, after the end of reconstruction, the original intention of the act was to prohibit federal troops from supervising elections in former Confederate states. More generally, the Posse Comitatus Act prohibits the use of the armed forces to execute the laws without congressional approval. For a more detailed history, see Wikipedia, s.vv. "Posse Comitatus Act," http://en.wikipedia.org/wiki/Posse_Comitatus_Act.

13. H.R. 5122, The John Warner National Defense Authorization Act for Fiscal Year 2007 § 1076(a)(1).

14. Originally martial law was imposed during wars or occupations to let the government control population more effectively in spite of heightened unrest. Nowadays it is most commonly used by authoritarian governments to enforce their rule. In a state of martial law, the military takes control of the ordinary administration of justice. In a country where martial law has been declared, a curfew is often imposed and the justice system is replaced by a military tribunal. The suspension of the writ of habeas corpus is likely to occur. See Wikipedia, s.vv., "Martial law."

15. George Orwell, *1984*, reissue ed. (Harcourt Brace Jovanovich, 1949; New York: New American Library, 1961), 267. Citations are to the 1961 edition.

CHAPTER 7

1. When they reached the West Wing, Card refused to allow Olson to enter his office. Comey relented and agreed to meet with Card alone. See next note.

2. "Senate Hearing on U.S. Attorney Firings, Part 1," CD Transcripts Wire, in WashingtonPost.com, May 15th 2007, http://www.washingtonpost.com /wp-dyn/content/article/2007/05/15/AR2007051501032.html.

3. Dan Eggen, "Official: Cheney Urged Wiretaps," *Washington Post,* June 7th 2007.

4. Michael J. Sniffen, "Ex-court Chief Criticizes Warrantless Eavesdropping," *Sunday Star-Ledger,* June 24th 2007.

5. From Orwell, *1984.* For a good outline of the novel and some of the history that led George Orwell to write it, see Wikipedia, s.vv., "Nineteen Eighty-Four."

6. Eric Lichtblau and James Risen, "Bush Lets US Spy on Callers Without Courts," *New York Times,* December 16th 2005.

7. *ACLU v. NSA* at 41, quoting Zweibon.

8. *ACLU v. NSA* at 24, quoting *Hamdi v. Rumsfeld.*

9. "'There Are No Hereditary Kings in America'—Judge Rules NSA Warrantless Spy Program Unconstitutional," *Democracy Now!* August 18th 2006, http://www.democracynow.org/article.pl?sid=06/08/18/1352240.

10. Brief for Appellant, http://www.aclu.org/pdfs/safefree/gov_appealbrief _6thcircuit.pdf, no longer available.

11. George W. Bush, "remarks by the president at independence day celebration, Independence Historic National Park, Philadelphia, Pennsylvania," http://www.priestsforlife.org/news/01-07-04bushjuly4.htm.

CHAPTER 8

1. Lara Jakes Jordan, "Justice Dept.: FBI Misused Patriot Act," Associated Press, March 9th 2007. Available online at http://www.breitbart.com/article .php?id=D8NOPCO02&show_article=1.

2. After the DOJ audit of the FBI use of NSLs went public, the Senate Judiciary Subcommittee on the Constitution needed someone to tell them what NSLs actually were. They called in Peter P. Swire and C. William O'Neill, professors of law at Moritz College of Law. For a very insightful history and outline of Patriot Act changes to NSLs, see "Use of National Security Letters by FBI," *Congressional Quarterly,* April 11th 2007.

3. USA Patriot Act H.R.3162 Sec 505(a)(3)(B).

4. Ibid., Sec 505(b)(1).

5. Federal Bureau of Investigation Web site, "FBI Executives," http://www.fbi .gov/libref/executives/asstmain.htm.

6. Eric Lichtblau and Marc Mazzetti, "Military Expands Intelligence Role in U.S." *New York Times,* January 14th 2007.

7. *Relevance* is a term that often arises with regard to the process of discovery in lawsuits. See *Federal Rules of Civil Procedure,* http://judiciary.house.gov /media/pdfs/printers/108th/civil2004.pdf.

8. For more of the DOJ's damning report, see U. S. Department of Justice, Office

of the Inspector General, *A Review of the Federal Bureau of Investigation's Use of National Security Letters*, March 2007, http://www.usdoj.gov/oig/special /s0703b/final.pdf.

9. *Doe v. Ashcroft* (2004), http://www.aclu.org/FilesPDFs/nsl_decision.pdf.

10. For a look at the actual National Security Letter, see http://www.aclu .org/images/nationalsecurityletters/asset_upload_file924_25995.pdf.

11. *Doe v. Gonzales* (2005), http://www.ctd.uscourts.gov/Opinions/090905 JCH.DoeOP.pdf.

12. For the full story see the anonymous editorial in the *Washington Post* entitled "My National Security Letter Gag Order," March 23rd 2007, A17.

CHAPTER 9

1. Judge Vaughn R. Walker, quoted in "Court Denies State Secrets Claim in Wiretapping Case," *Secrecy News*, http://www.fas.org/blog/secrecy/2006 /07/court_denies_state_secrets_cla_1.html, posted July 21st 2006.

2. Kevin Poulson, "Secrecy Power Sinks Patent Case," Wired.com, September 20th 2005, http://www.wired.com/science/discoveries/news/2005/09/68894.

CHAPTER 10

1. "Who's Watching?" A Special Report by the New York Civil Liberties Union, Fall 2006, http://www.nyclu.org/pdfs/surveillance_cams_report_121306.pdf.

2. Brad Hamilton, "Hidden Eyes of Our Apple," *New York Post*, May 2nd 2004.

3. Police officers and other government workers are essentially our employees, because the taxes we pay, whether property taxes, sales tax, or those taken out of our paychecks each week, go toward running our government on local and federal levels. Since when do the employees get to watch the employer? And why are the employers accepting this blatant disrespect from their employees when the employers are the ones responsible for every single employee's career?

4. Jim Dwyer, "New York Police Covertly Join In at Protest Rallies," *New York Times*, December 22nd 2005.

5. Ibid.

6. Dwyer, "Police Video Caught a Couple's Intimate Moment on a Manhattan Rooftop," *New York Times*, December 22nd 2005.

7. 18 U.S.C.A. § 1801, which states, "Whoever, in the special maritime and territorial jurisdiction of the United States, has the intent to capture an image of a private area of an individual without their consent, and knowingly does so under circumstances in which the individual has a reasonable expectation of privacy, shall be fined under this title or imprisoned not more than one year, or both."

8. States with Video Voyeurism Laws: Alaska, Arkansas, California, Connecticut, Delaware, Florida, Hawaii, Idaho, Illinois, Indiana, Kansas, Kentucky, Louisiana, Maine, Minnesota, New Jersey, New York, North Carolina, Ohio, Oklahoma, South Carolina, Tennessee, Texas, Utah, Virginia,

Washington, West Virginia, and Wisconsin, http://www.ncvc.org/src/AGP
.Net/Components/DocumentViewer/Download.aspxnz?DocumentID=37716.

9. McKinney's Penal Law § 250.45.

10. Dwyer, "Surveillance Prompts a Suit: Police v. Police," *New York Times*, February 3rd 2006.

11. Catherine Yang, "The State of Surveillance," *Business Week*, August 8th 2005.

12. Claudette Riley, "Overton County Schools Sued over Locker Room Filming," *Tennessean*. July 1st 2003, http://cgi.tennessean.com/cgi-bin/print/pr.pl.

13. Union Review, "Hidden Camera Footage Results in Worker Getting Fired," *Working Life*, June 24th 2007, http://www.workinglife.org/blogs/view_post .php?content_id=6674.

14. Randy Kenner, "Ohio Man Files $1.5 Million Suit Against Marriott: Hidden Camera Found in Bathroom," *Knoxville News Sentinel*, September 25th 2002, http://www.pvamu.edu/edir/wvetter/news/hotel-spy-camera-aug-02.doc; "Woman Sues Toys 'R' Us Over Hidden Camera," AP, July 11th 2003, http: //www.usatoday.com/tech/news/2003-07-11-toyruss-spycam_x.htm; "Man Sues over Bathroom Cameras," August 6th 2003, NBC6.net, http://www .nbc6.net/news/2387313/detail.html; E. J. Schultz, "Bar Defends Use of Men's Room Camera," *Island Packet*, October 18th 2003, http://www.island packet.com/news/local/story/2954566p-2710472c.html.

15. Thomas J. Jestel III, "Using Surveillance Camera Systems to Monitor Public Domains: Can Abuse Be Prevented?" (master's thesis, Naval Postgraduate School, Monterey, CA, March 2006), 6–7, http://stinet.dtic.mil/cgi-bin /GetTRDoc?AD=ADA445554&Location=U2&doc=GetTRDoc.pdf.

16. Sarah Wallace, "NYPD Housing Surveillance Staffed by Cops Under Investigation," WABC, April 23rd 2004, www.officer.com/article/printer.jsp ?id=12078&siteSection=1.

17. Ibid.

18. Ikimulisa Livingston, Philip Messing and Bill, "New York Police Seek Leak of Video," *New York Post*, April 1st 2004, http://www.officer.com/article /article.jsp?id=11339&siteSection=1.

19. Wallace, "NYPD Housing Surveillance Staffed by Cops."

20. "Three Arrested After Traffic Camera Aimed as [sic] Passersby," Associated Press, September 16th 2003, http://www.waff.com/Global/story.asp?S=144 5080.

21. Del Quentin Wilber and Derek Willis, "D.C. Red-Light Cameras Fail to Reduce Accidents," *Washington Post*, October 4th 2005, A01, http://www.washington post.com/wp-dyn/content/article/2005/10/03/AR2005 100301844.html.

22. Steven Brown (executive director, ACLU), letter to Mayor David Cicilline in Providence, RI, quoted in April 22nd 2003, http://www .aclu.org/pri-vacy/spying/15217prs20030422.html.

23. "Minnesota: Appeals Court Rules Against Cameras," September 25th 2006, http://www.thenewspaper.com/news/13/1356.asp.

24. "Texas DOT to Install Federally Funded Highway Speed Cameras," June 11th 2007, http://www.thenewspaper.com/news/18/1800.asp.

25. London's Ring of Steel is the secured area within the heart of London. By using video surveillance cameras, narrowed roadways, and roadblocks, officials are able to track every vehicle and person that enters the center of London and, when necessary, prevent them from entering and leaving the area.

26. William S. Sessions and Michael German, "Cameras Alone Won't Stop Crime," *Newark Star Ledger*, 2-1, August 19th 2007.

CHAPTER 11

1. "Airport Insecurity," *Seattle Times*, July 11–13th 2004, http://seattletimes .nwsource.com/news/nation-world/airportinsecurity/.

2. TSA quotations taken from *Seattle Times* article "TSA Denies Seizure of Sippy Cup," (Associated Press) June 17th 2007, http://seattletimes.nw source.com/html/nationworld/2003751103_tsacup17.html. Descriptions of incident taken from *USA Today* and Nowpublic.com.

3. Joe Sharkey, "Memo Pad," Business/Financial, *New York Times*, sec. C, August 7th 2007, late edition, final. The article is available online at http://select.nytimes .com/gst/abstract.html?res=F40916F83A540C748CDDA10894DF404482.

4. Yang, "The State of Surveillance."

5. Ibid.

6. Ibid.

7. Ibid.

8. "Iris on the Move," Sarnoff Corporation Web site, http://www.sarnoff.com /products_services/government_solutions/homeland_security/iris.asp.

9. There are federal and state laws in more than a dozen states (Alabama, New York, North Carolina, and Ohio, to name a few) that prohibit people from wearing a mask or disguise in public. See "Anti-Defamation League State Level Anti-Klan Statutory Provisions," July 2005, http://www.adl.org/learn /hate_crimes_laws/state_level_anti_klan_statutes.pdf.

10. "What's Respect About?" Respect Web site, http://www.respect.gov.uk/article .aspx?id=9054.

11. "Talking Cameras Berate Offenders," BBC, May 30th 2007, http://news.bbc .co.uk/2/hi/uk_news/england/merseyside/6706265.stm.

12. David Millward, "Airports to Track Passengers with Radio ID Tags," Telegraph.co.uk, http://www.telegraph.co.uk/news/main.jhtml?xml=/news /2007/04/10/nair10.xml.

13. "Who's Watching?" 7–9.

14. William Safire, "Nobody's Business," *New York Times*, January 8th 1998, viewable at http://www.cltg.org/cltg/privacy/98-01-08_Safire_Nobody's _Business.htm.

15. Simson L. Garfinkel, "Phone Calls Are Just the Start." *Washington Post*, May

14th 2006, B02, http://www.washingtonpost.com/wp-dyn/content/article/2006/05/13/AR2006051300043.html.

16. "Cell Phone 'Ping' Key to Finding Family," CBS News, December 6th 2006, http://wbztv.com/national/topstories_story_340085115.html.

17. Garfinkel, "Phone Calls Are Just the Start."

18. Yang, "The State of Surveillance."

19. "FBI Apologizes to Lawyer Held in Madrid Bombings," Associated Press, May 25th 2004, http://www.msnbc.msn.com/id/5053007/.

CHAPTER 12

1. The loose term used to refer to members of the armed forces of the state with which another state is at war (aka "prisoners of war"). It is important to note the distinction between "enemy combatants" and "unlawful enemy combatants"; unlawful combatants are nonuniformed fighters who, according to the Bush administration, are not entitled to the prisoner-of-war status.

2. Full debate and legislative history available at Wikipedia.com, s.vv., "Military Commissions Act of 2006."

3. S. 3930 MCA06 Sec 948b.

4. S. 3930 Sec 948d.

5. Ibid, subsection i.

6. George W. Bush, in Address to a Joint Session of Congress and the American People, September 2001, http://www.whitehouse.gov/news/releases/2001/09/20010920-8.html.

7. Adam Liptak, "U.S. Court Says Military Can't detain Civilians Indefinitely," *International Herald Tribune*, June 12th 2007, http://www.iht.com/articles/2007/06/12/frontpage/court.php.

8. 69 FR 31291—Appointing Authority for Military Commissions.

9. To date, there are only male detainees at Gitmo. I say "he or she" here to emphasize the future possibility that anyone can be labeled an unlawful enemy combatant.

10. S.3930 Military Commissions Act 2006, Sec. 949c.

11. Executive Order 12968.

12. S.3930 Military Commissions Act 2006, Sec. 949d.

CHAPTER 13

1. Geneva III, art. 17, provides that no physical or mental torture, nor any other form of coercion, may be inflicted on prisoners of war to secure from them information of any kind whatever. Geneva prohibits violence to life and person, mutilation, cruel treatment and torture, outrages upon personal dignity, and, in particular, humiliating and degrading treatment.

2. Barton Gellman and Jo Becker, "Pushing the Envelope on Presidential Power," *Washington Post*, June 25th 2007, http://blog.washingtonpost.com/cheney/chapters/pushing_the_envelope_on_presi/index.html.

3. 18 USC § 2441: "Whoever, whether inside or outside the United States, commits a war crime . . . shall be fined under this title or imprisoned for life or any term of years, or both, and if death results to the victim, shall also be subject to the death penalty."

4. Mike Allen and Dana Priest, "Memo on Torture Draws Focus to Bush," *Washington Post*, June 9th 2004, A03, http://www.washingtonpost.com /wp-dyn/articles/A26401-2004Jun8.html.

5. The entire text is available at http://frwebgate.access.gpo.gov/cgi-bin/ getdoc .cgi?dbname=109_cong_bills&docid=f:s3930enr.txt.pdf.

6. Anne Applebaum, "The Torture Myth," *Washington Post*, January 12th 2005, A21, http://www.washingtonpost.com/wp-dyn/articles/A2302-2005Jan11 .html.

7. Brian Ross and Richard Esposito, "CIA's Harsh Interrogation Techniques Described," ABC News, November 18th 2005, http://abcnews.go.com/WNT /Investigation/story?id=1322866.

8. According to CIA sources cited in Brian Ross's ABC interview, the prisoner is bound to an inclined board, feet raised and head slightly below the feet. Cellophane is wrapped over the prisoner's face, and water is poured over him. Unavoidably, the gag reflex kicks in, and a terrifying fear of drowning leads to almost instant pleas to bring the treatment to a halt. According to the sources, CIA officers who subjected themselves to the waterboarding technique lasted an average of fourteen seconds before caving in. They said al-Qaeda's toughest prisoner, Khalid Sheik Mohammed, won the admiration of interrogators when he was able to last between two and two and a half minutes before begging to confess.

9. "FBI Documented Possible Gitmo Mistreatment," CBS News, January 3rd 2007, http://www.cbsnews.com/stories/2007/01/02/terror/main23248 19.shtml.

10. Dana Priest, "Wrongful Imprisonment: Anatomy of a CIA Mistake," *Washington Post*, December 4th 2005, A01,http://www.washingtonpost.com /wp-dyn/content/article/2005/12/03/AR2005120301476.html.

11. Luke Harding, "CIA's Secret Jails Open Up New Transatlantic Rift," *Guardian*, December 5th 2005, http://www.guardian.co.uk/usa/story/0,,16 57839,00.html.

12. PDD 39, U.S. Policy on Counterterrorism, June 21st 1995, http://www .fas.org/irp/offdocs/pdd39.htm.

13. "EU Countries Ignored Terror Suspect Flights, Report Says," *Guardian Unlimited*, February 14th 2007, http://www.guardian.co.uk/usa/story/0,,20 12966,00.html.

14. "Fact Sheet: Extraordinary Rendition," ACLU, November 6th 2005, http: //www.aclu.org/safefree/extraordinaryrendition/22203res20051206 .html.

15. Ian Cobain, "Seized, Held, Tortured: Six Tell Same Tale," *Guardian*,

December 6th 2005, http://www.guardian.co.uk/usa/story/0,,1659302,00.html.

16. Craig S. Smith and Souad Mekhennet, "Algerian Tells of Dark Term in U.S. Hands," *New York Times*, July 7th 2006, http://www.nytimes.com/2006/07/07/world/africa/07algeria.html?ei=5090&en=17b76be0aba70618&ex=1309924800&partner=rssuserland&emc=rss&pagewanted=all.

17. "Off the Record: U.S. Responsibility for Enforced Disappearances in the 'War on Terror'" June 2007, available at http://hrw.org/backgrounder/usa/ct0607/.

18. Boeing Web site, http://www.boeing.com/commercial/flightops/itp.html.

19. Jane Mayer, "Outsourcing: The C.I.A.'s Travel Agent," *New Yorker*, October 30th 2006, http://www.newyorker.com/archive/2006/10/30/061030ta_talk_mayer.

20. Ibid.

21. "US Judge Dismisses Torture Case for National Security Reasons," Reuters, May 19th 2006, http://www.abc.net.au/news/newsitems/200605/s1642842.htm.

CHAPTER 14

1. "To those who scare peace-loving people with phantoms of lost liberty, my message is this: Your tactics only aid terrorists, for they erode our national unity and diminish our resolve. They give ammunition to America's enemies, and pause to America's friends," John Ashcroft, in Jacob Weisburg, "Ashcroft Deconstructed," *Slate*, December 7th 2001, http://www.slate.com/?id=2059538.

2. Eric Alterman, "'Objectivity' RIP," *Nation*, December 24th 2001, http://www.thenation.com/doc/20011224/alterman.

3. *World News Tonight* with Charles Gibson, May 22nd 2007.

4. David Bauder, "Romney: ABC Story Puts Lives at Risk," *USA Today*, May 23rd 2007, http://www.usatoday.com/news/politics/2007-05-23-2551907064_x.htm.

5. Dante Chinni, "National Security vs. Freedom of the Press: The Media Must Monitor the Powerful, Not Just Serve as Their Mouthpiece," *Christian Science Monitor*, May 23rd 2006, http://www.commondreams.org/views06/0523-32.htm.

6. Charles Adams, "The Land of the Not-So Free," LewRockwell.com, Associated Press, May 14nd 2007, http://www.lewrockwell.com/adams/adams12.html.

7. "Gonzales: Reporters Can Be Prosecuted for Revealing Classified Info," May 22, 2006, http://www.firstamendmentcenter.org/news .aspx?id=16921.

8. Committee to Protect Journalists, "Panel Raises Concerns About Journalists Held Without Charge by U.S.," May 8th 2007, http://www.cpj.org/news/2007/americas/usa08may07na.html.

9. Gil Kaufman, with reporting by Gideon Yago, "Iraq Uploaded: The War

Network TV Won't Show You, Shot by Soldiers and Posted Online," MTV Web site, July 20th 2006, http://www.mtv.com/news/articles/1536780/2006 0720/index.jhtml.

10. Noah Schactman, "Army Squeezes Soldier Blogs, Maybe to Death," *Wired,* May 2nd 2007, http://www.wired.com/politics/onlinerights/news/2007/05 /army_bloggers.

11. Ibid.

12. Maj. Pam Newbern, "Virginia National Guard Eyes Web Sites, Blogs," Army News Service, October 12th 2006, ARNEWS Web site, http://www4.army .mil/OCPA/read.php?story_id_key=9707.

13. Alan Sipress and Sam Diaz, "A Casuality of War: MySpace," *Washington Post,* May 15th 2007, A01, http://www.washingtonpost.com/wp-dyn/content /article/2007/05/14/AR2007051400112.html.

14. Ibid.

15. Nikki Schwab, "Military Bloggers Wary of New Policy," *Washington Post,* May 5th 2007, http://www.washingtonpost.com/wp-dyn/content/article/2007/05 /05/AR2007050500881.html.

CHAPTER 15

1. Tom Moran, "For a Desperate City, a Defining Moment," *Star-Ledger* (Newark, NJ), August 8th 2007, and at NJ.com, http://www.nj.com /columns/ledger/moran/index.ssf?/base/columns-0/1186549321219510 .xml&coll=1#continue.

2. *Olmstead v. United States,* 277 U.S. 438.

INDEX

APPENDIX

INTRODUCTION TO THE U.S. CONSTITUTION

The Constitution of the United States is the most examined and debated document in our country's history. It was written as a classic American compromise after months of debate at the Constitutional Convention in Philadelphia, which met during the summer of 1787. Essentially, the document constructs, establishes, and imposes limitations on the federal government by which each of the states gave some of their independent sovereign power away and created a new central government.

THE GREAT COMPROMISE

The Constitution was not the first effort by the states to create a central government. The first effort was the Articles of Confederation. Basically it created an umbrella government, subject to the wishes of the various states, any one of which could disregard a law that the central government enacted. Because of fears that Great Britain, the country from which our colonies broke away, would some day attempt to take back the states—a fear which, of course, came true in 1812—many political leaders felt the Articles of Confederation did not provide the type of central government strong enough to unite the former colonies into one sovereign capable of dealing with all foreign governments with one voice, and strong enough to protect its people.

The Constitution is unique because it indisputably establishes the primacy of the individual over the state. It guarantees liberties and guarantees that the central government will not impair them. Basically, the Constitution is the result of a compromise between Federalists personified by Alexander Hamilton, who wanted a very strong central government, and Anti-Federalists personified by Thomas Jefferson, who wanted strict limitations on the new government's powers and guarantees of liberty. Thus, out of that conflict of ideas, the federal government was born.

THE PRESIDENCY

The Constitution provides for a strong chief executive—not a king—but an executive who is not subject to either of the two branches. What do I mean by this? In the modern European system, the head of the government is the prime minister. The prime minister is also the head of the political party that dominates the legislative branch. The prime minister of most modern European countries is not elected in a popular vote. His parties' representatives are elected to parliament and, if they have a majority in parliament, they choose him as the leader of their party to become the leader of the government. The prime minister's name does not appear on a national ballot as a candidate for that office.

Here in the U.S., of course, the president, though voted for popularly, actually is chosen by electors from the states where the voters chose him. The people vote in each state directly for electors, and the electors promise they will cast their state's electoral votes for the winner of that state's popular vote. Usually the person who wins the national popular vote becomes president; but as the 2000 election exemplified, that is not always the case.

Nevertheless, the Constitution gives us a strong chief executive, not one whose powers derive from the legislature, but one whose powers derive from the Constitution. If a British prime minister loses a vote of confidence, that is, if Parliament rejects one of his proposals, he can be swept from office and forced to stand for re-election; not so with the American president. Not only may he lose a vote in the Congress and still keep his job, but he doesn't even have to be in the same party as that which dominates Congress, and frequently that has been the case.

THE LEGISLATURE

The Congress was created by the Constitution to represent the states and the people. Originally, senators were not popularly elected, but rather elected by state legislatures for six-year terms. Thus, the senators didn't represent the people in a state, they represented the state itself, its government, its sovereignty, in the United States Senate. In 1913, the Constitution was amended to provide for direct popular election of senators.

Members of the House of Representatives have always been popularly elected. The House has always been considered "the peoples' house," and its representatives seek re-election every two years.

Thus, in the two popular branches of government, we see a classic American compromise. In the Senate are representatives of the sovereign states. In the House of Representatives are representatives of the people. In the presidency is a person who must have broad popular support but could actually be elected without it.

THE JUDICIARY

The most peculiar branch, and the least understood, is the judiciary. The judicial branch of the government consists of life-tenured judges appointed by the president and confirmed by the Senate. These judges, of course, never have to seek election and can only be removed from office upon impeachment, after conviction of a felony.

The purpose of the judicial branch, as created by the Constitution, was to hear trials and apply federal laws to the unique cases before them. In the very famous case of *Marbury v. Madison*, however, in 1803, the

Supreme Court decided that its purpose would be grander than that. The Court claimed for itself the power to invalidate acts of the Congress which were inconsistent with the Constitution. At the time, such power was considered a radical notion.

William Marbury had been appointed as a federal magistrate by outgoing President John Adams, a Federalist. His appointment was confirmed by the Senate, but the secretary of state in the Adams administration neglected to give Marbury his formal commission. After Thomas Jefferson, an Anti-Federalist, became president, his secretary of state, James Madison, refused to deliver Marbury his commission. So Marbury sued Madison in the Supreme Court seeking an order to compel Madison to deliver the commission to Marbury. The Supreme Court rejected Marbury's claim, not because he was not entitled to it (he was), but because the Congressional statute under which he sued, which gave the Supreme Court original jurisdiction over this type of lawsuit, was unconstitutional. This was so, the Court ruled, because the Constitution dictates the areas over which the Supreme Court has original jurisdiction, and the Congress cannot alter that. The party that immediately benefited by the outcome of *Marbury v. Madison* was the Anti-Federalists, who were in power at the time, and the result—that Mr. Marbury did not become a magistrate—was then popular. But of course, this power would dog presidents and congresses even up to the present day.

The power is called "judicial review," and it is now universally accepted that not only the Supreme Court, but all federal judges, can review and void acts of Congress or acts of the president which the federal judge is able to demonstrate are inconsistent with the Constitution. For example, if the president were to declare that he did not need to seek reelection and he was entitled to retain his job for life, and a lawsuit were filed challenging that declaration, it would be easy for a federal judge to invalidate the declaration because it is inconsistent with the Constitution which sets the president's term at four years. If Congress were to enact a law that made it unlawful to criticize members of the Congress, it would be easy for a federal judge to invalidate that law as inconsistent with the First Amendment to the Constitution, which guarantees freedom of speech.

I have addressed judicial review at length in this book. It is indeed controversial, but now nearly universally accepted. Sometimes we call the exercise of judicial review judicial activism when we disagree with what the court does; sometimes we call it judicial heroism when we agree with the judicial outcome.

THE BILL OF RIGHTS

The amendments to the Constitution are divided into two categories. The first ten of them are known as the Bill of Rights.

The Bill of Rights was promised to Thomas Jefferson and the Anti-Federalists as a condition for their support for the Constitution. The great fear of the Anti-Federalists—those who if around today would fear Big Government—was that the central government would take personal liberty away from individuals and power away from the states. When the authors of the Constitution guaranteed the Anti-Federalists that the document would contain a Bill of Rights which would spell out the rights and liberties that the Constitution would guarantee, and would retain powers for the states, it was an easier sell in those states concerned about personal freedom and limited government.

When we use the term the Bill of Rights, we are referring only to the first ten amendments to the Constitution. If you read those ten amendments, you will see that they consist of guaranteeing specific individual rights that the federal government cannot take away, and powers that the states will always keep.

After we fought the Civil War, and added the Thirteenth, Fourteenth, and Fifteenth Amendments, the courts began interpreting those, especially the Fourteenth, as meaning that not only can the federal government not interfere with liberties guaranteed in the Bill of Rights, but also, none of the state governments can interfere with them either.

STATE SOVEREIGNTY

The starting point of the Constitution is that the thirteen states which formed the federal government were sovereign and independent states free to go their own way. There was a Continental Congress, of course, in 1776. It had little or no power other than to direct then General George Washington as he waged war against the British. The real political power that existed in 1776 was in the governorship and the legislature of each of the thirteen states.

When those political leaders of those thirteen states agreed that the Articles of Confederation were too weak to allow the country to be perceived as a sovereign unit by foreign countries, each of the states gave away some of their power to form the new central government.

Even though the Constitution begins with "We the people," it was really "We the States" that formed the Constitution. The Constitution itself indicates that it would not come into existence until two thirds of the thirteen states agreed to accept it. So when one thinks of the federal government of the United States of America, one should think of a government with limitations imposed on it by the Constitution and with powers given to it by the various states. This, of course, presumes, and historically this is the case, that the thirteen original states preceded the existence of the federal government and actually, literally gave away some of their powers so as to form a central government. As an example, before 1789, many states issued their own currency and had their own armies. This obviously is something they cannot do under the Constitution because they gave those powers away to the central, federal government.

SEPARATION OF POWERS

The Constitution itself divides power, as we saw earlier, among a president who enforces the laws, a Congress which writes the laws, and a judiciary which interprets the laws. It also, of course, limits the powers of the three branches of government so that they deal with problems that are truly federal in nature. Unfortunately, these limitations have rarely been honored, and throughout the many years of our existence, fanatics and busybodies, do-gooders and collectivists in the congresses have found infamous and duplicitous ways, and power-hungry judges in the courts have bent over backward to allow congresses and presidents, to exercise power never contemplated by the Constitution.

Article 1, section 8 specifically lists only eighteen areas of human behavior over which Congress may legislate, and thus the president may enforce, and the courts may interpret. Those areas involve coining money, regulating interstate and foreign commerce, establishing rules of naturalization, establishing post offices and courts, and supporting an army and navy. The power to regulate all other areas of human behavior that the Natural Law allows governments to regulate was retained by the States. Despite the strict enumeration of congressional powers, the Congress has exercised powers never granted, enumerated, or delegated to it and has regulated, with the courts' approval, everything from automobile speed limits to the amount of sugar in ketchup, from the size of toilet bowls to the wages of janitors, from the fat content of cheese to the number of lobsters you can catch and the amount of wheat you can grow, from the number of pain killers your physician can prescribe to the amount of your income you can keep.

Jefferson and Madison would not be happy with what's become of it, but here is the Constitution, with the Bill of Rights and the other amendments, in all its simple glory. While I've largely left alone the style elements peculiar to when the Constitution was written, I have updated the spellings of a few words for easier readability.

THE CONSTITUTION OF THE UNITED STATES

We the People of the United States, in Order to form a more perfect Union, establish Justice, insure domestic Tranquility, provide for the common defense, promote the general Welfare, and secure the Blessings of Liberty to ourselves and our Posterity, do ordain and establish this Constitution for the United States of America.

ARTICLE 1

Section 1. All legislative Powers herein granted shall be vested in a Congress of the United States, which shall consist of a Senate and House of Representatives.

Section 2. The House of Representatives shall be composed of Members chosen every second Year by the People of the several States, and the Electors in each State shall have the Qualifications requisite for Electors of the most numerous Branch of the State Legislature.

No Person shall be a Representative who shall not have attained to the Age of twenty five Years, and been seven Years a Citizen of the United States, and who shall not, when elected, be an Inhabitant of that State in which he shall be chosen.

Representatives and direct Taxes shall be apportioned among the several States which may be included within this Union, according to their respective Numbers, which shall be determined by adding to the whole Number of free Persons, including those bound to Service for a Term of Years, and excluding Indians not taxed, three fifths of all other Persons.[1] The actual Enumeration shall be made within three Years after the first Meeting of the Congress of the United States, and within every subsequent Term of ten Years, in such Manner as they shall by Law direct. The Number of Representatives shall not exceed one for every thirty Thousand, but each State shall have at Least one Representative; and until such enumeration shall be made, the State of New Hampshire shall be entitled to choose three, Massachusetts eight, Rhode-Island and Providence Plantations one, Connecticut five, New-York six, New Jersey four, Pennsylvania eight, Delaware one, Maryland six, Virginia ten, North Carolina five, South Carolina five, and Georgia three.

When vacancies happen in the Representation from any State,

the Executive Authority thereof shall issue Writs of Election to fill such Vacancies.

The House of Representatives shall choose their Speaker and other Officers; and shall have the sole Power of Impeachment.

Section 3. The Senate of the United States shall be composed of two Senators from each State, chosen by the Legislature[2] thereof for six Years; and each Senator shall have one Vote.

Immediately after they shall be assembled in Consequence of the first Election, they shall be divided as equally as may be into three Classes. The Seats of the Senators of the first Class shall be vacated at the Expiration of the second Year, of the second Class at the Expiration of the fourth Year, and of the third Class at the Expiration of the sixth Year, so that one third may be chosen every second Year; and if Vacancies happen by Resignation, or otherwise, during the Recess of the Legislature of any State, the Executive thereof may make temporary Appointments until the next Meeting of the Legislature, which shall then fill such Vacancies.[3]

No Person shall be a Senator who shall not have attained to the Age of thirty Years, and been nine Years a Citizen of the United States, and who shall not, when elected, be an Inhabitant of that State for which he shall be chosen.

The Vice President of the United States shall be President of the Senate, but shall have no Vote, unless they be equally divided.

The Senate shall choose their other Officers, and also a President pro tempore, in the Absence of the Vice President, or when he shall exercise the Office of President of the United States.

The Senate shall have the sole Power to try all Impeachments. When sitting for that Purpose, they shall be on Oath or Affirmation. When the President of the United States is tried, the Chief Justice shall preside: And no Person shall be convicted without the Concurrence of two thirds of the Members present.

Judgment in Cases of Impeachment shall not extend further than to removal from Office, and disqualification to hold and enjoy any Office of honor, Trust or Profit under the United States: but the Party convicted shall nevertheless be liable and subject to Indictment, Trial, Judgment and Punishment, according to Law.

Section 4. The Times, Places and Manner of holding Elections for Senators and Representatives, shall be prescribed in each State by the Legislature thereof; but the Congress may at any time by Law make or alter such Regulations, except as to the Places of choosing Senators.

The Congress shall assemble at least once in every Year, and such Meeting shall be on the first Monday in December,[4] unless they shall by Law appoint a different Day.

Section 5. Each House shall be the Judge of the Elections, Returns and Qualifications of its own Members, and a Majority of each shall constitute a Quorum to do Business; but a smaller Number may adjourn from day to day, and may be authorized to compel the Attendance of absent Members, in such Manner, and under such Penalties as each House may provide.

Each House may determine the Rules of its Proceedings, punish its Members for disorderly Behavior, and, with the Concurrence of two thirds, expel a Member.

Each House shall keep a Journal of its Proceedings, and from time to time publish the same, excepting such Parts as may in their Judgment require Secrecy; and the Yeas and Nays of the Members of either House on any question shall, at the Desire of one fifth of those Present, be entered on the Journal.

Neither House, during the Session of Congress, shall, without the Consent of the other, adjourn for more than three days, nor to any other Place than that in which the two Houses shall be sitting.

Section 6. The Senators and Representatives shall receive a Compensation for their Services, to be ascertained by Law, and paid out of the Treasury of the United States. They shall in all Cases, except Treason, Felony and Breach of the Peace, be privileged from Arrest during their Attendance at the Session of their respective Houses, and in going to and returning from the same; and for any Speech or Debate in either House, they shall not be questioned in any other Place.

No Senator or Representative shall, during the Time for which he was elected, be appointed to any civil Office under the Authority of the United States, which shall have been created, or the Emoluments whereof shall have been increased during such time; and no Person holding any Office under the United States, shall be a Member of either House during his Continuance in Office.

Section 7. All Bills for raising Revenue shall originate in the House of Representatives; but the Senate may propose or concur with Amendments as on other Bills.

Every Bill which shall have passed the House of Representatives and the Senate, shall, before it become a Law, be presented to the President of the United States: If he approve he shall sign it, but if not he shall return it, with his Objections to that House in which it shall have originated, who shall enter the Objections at large on their Journal, and proceed to reconsider it. If after such Reconsideration two thirds of that House shall agree to pass the Bill, it shall be sent, together with the Objections, to the other House, by which it shall likewise be reconsidered, and if approved by two thirds of that House, it shall become a Law. But in all such Cases the Votes of both Houses shall be determined by Yeas and Nays, and the Names of the Persons voting for and against the Bill shall be entered on the Journal of each House respectively. If any Bill shall not be returned by the President within ten Days (Sundays excepted) after it shall have been presented to him, the Same shall be a Law, in like Manner as if he had signed it, unless the Congress by their Adjournment prevent its Return, in which Case it shall not be a Law.

Every Order, Resolution, or Vote to which the Concurrence of the Senate and House of Representatives may be necessary (except on a question of Adjournment) shall be presented to the President of the United States; and before the Same shall take Effect, shall be approved by him, or being disapproved by him, shall be repassed by two thirds of the Senate and House of Representatives, according to the Rules and Limitations prescribed in the Case of a Bill.

Section 8. The Congress shall have Power To lay and collect Taxes, Duties, Imposts and Excises, to pay the Debts and provide for the common Defense and general Welfare of the United States; but all Duties, Imposts and Excises shall be uniform throughout the United States;

To borrow Money on the credit of the United States;

To regulate Commerce with foreign Nations, and among the several States, and with the Indian Tribes;

To establish an uniform Rule of Naturalization, and uniform Laws on the subject of Bankruptcies throughout the United States;

To coin Money, regulate the Value thereof, and of foreign Coin, and fix the Standard of Weights and Measures;

To provide for the Punishment of counterfeiting the Securities and current Coin of the United States;

To establish Post Offices and post Roads;

To promote the Progress of Science and useful Arts, by securing for limited Times to Authors and Inventors the exclusive Right to their respective Writings and Discoveries;

To constitute Tribunals inferior to the supreme Court;

To define and punish Piracies and Felonies committed on the high Seas, and Offences against the Law of Nations;

To declare War, grant Letters of Marque and Reprisal, and make Rules concerning Captures on Land and Water;

To raise and support Armies, but no Appropriation of Money to that Use shall be for a longer Term than two Years;

To provide and maintain a Navy;

To make Rules for the Government and Regulation of the land and naval Forces;

To provide for calling forth the Militia to execute the Laws of the Union, suppress Insurrections and repel Invasions;

To provide for organizing, arming, and disciplining the Militia, and for governing such Part of them as may be employed in the Service of the United States, reserving to the States respectively, the Appointment of the Officers, and the Authority of training the Militia according to the discipline prescribed by Congress;

To exercise exclusive Legislation in all Cases whatsoever, over such District (not exceeding ten Miles square) as may, by Cession of particular States, and the Acceptance of Congress, become the Seat of the Government of the United States, and to exercise like Authority over all Places purchased by the Consent of the Legislature of the State in which the Same shall be, for the Erection of Forts, Magazines, Arsenals, dock-Yards, and other needful Buildings;—And

To make all Laws which shall be necessary and proper for carry-ing into Execution the foregoing Powers, and all other Powers vested by this Constitution in the Government of the United States, or in any Department or Officer thereof.

Section 9. The Migration or Importation of such Persons as any of the States now existing shall think proper to admit, shall not be prohibited by the Congress prior to the Year one thousand eight hundred and eight, but a Tax or duty may be imposed on such Importation, not exceeding ten dollars for each Person.

The Privilege of the Writ of Habeas Corpus shall not be suspended, unless when in Cases of Rebellion or Invasion the public Safety may require it.

No Bill of Attainder or ex post facto Law shall be passed.

No Capitation, or other direct, Tax shall be laid, unless in Proportion to the Census or enumeration herein before directed to be taken.[5]

No Tax or Duty shall be laid on Articles exported from any State.

No Preference shall be given by any Regulation of Commerce or Revenue to the Ports of one State over those of another; nor shall Vessels bound to, or from, one State, be obliged to enter, clear, or pay Duties in another.

No Money shall be drawn from the Treasury, but in Consequence of Appropriations made by Law; and a regular Statement and Account of the Receipts and Expenditures of all public Money shall be published from time to time.

No Title of Nobility shall be granted by the United States. And no Person holding any Office of Profit or Trust under them, shall, without the Consent of the Congress, accept of any present, Emolument, Office, or Title, of any kind whatever, from any King, Prince, or foreign State.

Section 10. No State shall enter into any Treaty, Alliance, or Confederation; grant Letters of Marque and Reprisal; coin Money; emit Bills of Credit; make any Thing but gold and silver Coin a Tender in Payment of Debts; pass any Bill of Attainder, ex post facto Law, or Law impairing the Obligation of Contracts, or grant any Title of Nobility.

No State shall, without the Consent of the Congress, lay any Imposts or Duties on Imports or Exports, except what may be absolutely necessary for executing its inspection Laws: and the net Produce of all Duties and Imposts, laid by any State on Imports or Exports, shall be for the Use of the Treasury of the United States; and all such Laws shall be subject to the Revision and Control of the Congress.

No State shall, without the Consent of Congress, lay any Duty of Tonnage, keep Troops, or Ships of War in time of Peace, enter into any Agreement or Compact with another State, or with a foreign Power, or engage in War, unless actually invaded, or in such imminent Danger as will not admit of delay.

ARTICLE 2

Section 1. The executive Power shall be vested in a President of the United States of America. He shall hold his Office during the Term of four Years, and, together with the Vice President, chosen for the same Term, be elected, as follows:

Each State shall appoint, in such Manner as the Legislature thereof may direct, a Number of Electors, equal to the whole Number of Senators and Representatives to which the State may be entitled in the Congress: but no Senator or Representative, or Person holding an Office of Trust or Profit under the United States, shall be appointed an Elector.

The Electors shall meet in their respective States, and vote by Ballot for two Persons, of whom one at least shall not be an Inhabitant of the same State with themselves. And they shall make a List of all the Persons voted for, and of the Number of Votes for each; which List they shall sign and certify, and transmit sealed to the Seat of the Government of the United States, directed to the President of the Senate. The President of the Senate shall, in the Presence of the Senate and House of Representatives, open all the Certificates, and the Votes shall then be counted. The Person having the greatest Number of Votes shall be the President, if such Number be a Majority of the whole Number of Electors appointed; and if there be more than one who have such Majority, and have an equal Number of Votes, then the House of Representatives shall immediately choose by Ballot one of them for President; and if no Person have a Majority, then from the five highest on the List the said House shall in like Manner choose the President. But in choosing the President, the Votes shall be taken by States, the Representation from each State having one Vote; A quorum for this purpose shall consist of a Member or Members from two thirds of the States, and a Majority of all the States shall be necessary to a Choice. In every Case, after the Choice of the President, the Person having the greatest Number of Votes of the Electors shall be the Vice President. But if there should remain two or more who have equal Votes, the Senate shall choose from them by Ballot the Vice President.[6]

The Congress may determine the Time of choosing the Electors, and the Day on which they shall give their Votes; which Day shall be the same throughout the United States.

No Person except a natural born Citizen, or a Citizen of the United States, at the time of the Adoption of this Constitution, shall be eligible to the Office of President; neither shall any Person be eligible to that Office who shall not have attained to the Age of thirty five Years, and been fourteen Years a Resident within the United States.

In Case of the Removal of the President from Office, or of his Death, Resignation, or Inability to discharge the Powers and Duties of the said Office, the Same shall devolve on the Vice President, and the Congress may by Law provide for the Case of Removal, Death, Resignation or Inability, both of the President and Vice President, declaring what Officer shall then act as President, and such Officer shall act accordingly, until the Disability be removed, or a President shall be elected.[7]

The President shall, at stated Times, receive for his Services, a Compensation, which shall neither be increased nor diminished during the Period for which he shall have been elected, and he shall not receive within that Period any other Emolument from the United States, or any of them.

Before he enters on the Execution of his Office, he shall take the following Oath or Affirmation:—"I do solemnly swear (or affirm) that I will faithfully execute the Office of President of the United States, and will to the best of my Ability, preserve, protect and defend the Constitution of the United States."

Section 2. The President shall be Commander in Chief of the Army and Navy of the United States, and of the Militia of the several States, when called into the actual Service of the United States; he may require the Opinion, in writing, of the principal Officer in each of the executive Departments, upon any Subject relating to the Duties of their respective Offices, and he shall have Power to grant Reprieves and Pardons for Offences against the United States, except in Cases of Impeachment.

He shall have Power, by and with the Advice and Consent of the Senate, to make Treaties, provided two thirds of the Senators present concur; and he shall nominate, and by and with the Advice and Consent of the Senate, shall appoint Ambassadors, other public Ministers and Consuls, Judges of the supreme Court, and all other Officers of the United States, whose Appointments are not herein otherwise provided for, and which shall be established by Law: but the Congress may by Law vest the Appointment of such inferior Officers, as they think proper, in the President alone, in the Courts of Law, or in the Heads of Departments.

The President shall have Power to fill up all Vacancies that may happen during the Recess of the Senate, by granting Commissions which shall expire at the End of their next Session.

Section 3. He shall from time to time give to the Congress Information of the State of the Union, and recommend to their Consideration such Measures as he shall judge necessary and expedient; he may, on extraordinary Occasions, convene both Houses, or either of them, and in Case of Disagreement between them, with Respect to the Time of Adjournment, he may adjourn them to such Time as he shall think proper; he shall receive Ambassadors and other public Ministers; he shall take Care that the Laws be faithfully executed, and shall Commission all the Officers of the United States.

Section 4. The President, Vice President and all civil Officers of the United States, shall be removed from Office on Impeachment for, and Conviction of, Treason, Bribery, or other high Crimes and Misdemeanors.

Article 3

Section 1. The judicial Power of the United States shall be vested in one supreme Court, and in such inferior Courts as the Congress may from time to time ordain and establish. The Judges, both of the supreme and inferior Courts, shall hold their Offices during good Behavior, and shall, at stated Times, receive for their Services a Compensation, which shall not be diminished during their Continuance in Office.

Section 2. The judicial Power shall extend to all Cases, in Law and Equity, arising under this Constitution, the Laws of the United States, and Treaties made, or which shall be made, under their Authority;—to all Cases affecting Ambassadors, other public Ministers and Consuls;—to all Cases of admiralty and maritime Jurisdiction;—to Controversies to which the United States shall be a Party;—to Controversies between two or more States;—between a State and Citizens of another State[8];—between Citizens of different States;—between Citizens of the same State claiming Lands under Grants of different States, and between a State, or the Citizens thereof, and foreign States, Citizens or Subjects.

In all Cases affecting Ambassadors, other public Ministers and Consuls, and those in which a State shall be Party, the supreme Court shall have original Jurisdiction. In all the other Cases before mentioned, the supreme Court shall have appellate Jurisdiction, both as to Law and Fact, with such Exceptions, and under such Regulations as the Congress shall make.

The Trial of all Crimes, except in Cases of Impeachment, shall be by Jury; and such Trial shall be held in the State where the said Crimes shall have been committed; but when not committed within any State, the Trial shall be at such Place or Places as the Congress may by Law have directed.

Section 3. Treason against the United States, shall consist only in levying War against them, or in adhering to their Enemies, giving them Aid and Comfort. No Person shall be convicted of Treason unless on the Testimony of two Witnesses to the same overt Act, or on Confession in open Court.

The Congress shall have Power to declare the Punishment of Treason, but no Attainder of Treason shall work Corruption of Blood, or Forfeiture except during the Life of the Person attainted.

ARTICLE 4

Section 1. Full Faith and Credit shall be given in each State to the public Acts, Records, and judicial Proceedings of every other State.

And the Congress may by general Laws prescribe the Manner in which such Acts, Records and Proceedings shall be proved, and the Effect thereof.

Section 2. The Citizens of each State shall be entitled to all Privileges and Immunities of Citizens in the several States.

A Person charged in any State with Treason, Felony, or other Crime, who shall flee from Justice, and be found in another State, shall on Demand of the executive Authority of the State from which he fled, be delivered up, to be removed to the State having Jurisdiction of the Crime.

No Person held to Service or Labor in one State, under the Laws thereof, escaping into another, shall, in Consequence of any Law or Regulation therein, be discharged from such Service or Labor, but shall be delivered up on Claim of the Party to whom such Service or Labor may be due.[9]

Section 3. New States may be admitted by the Congress into this Union; but no new State shall be formed or erected within the Jurisdiction of any other State; nor any State be formed by the Junction of two or more States, or Parts of States, without the Consent of the Legislatures of the States concerned as well as of the Congress.

The Congress shall have Power to dispose of and make all needful Rules and Regulations respecting the Territory or other Property belonging to the United States; and nothing in this Constitution shall be so construed as to Prejudice any Claims of the United States, or of any particular State.

Section 4. The United States shall guarantee to every State in this Union a Republican Form of Government, and shall protect each of them against Invasion; and on Application of the Legislature, or of the Executive (when the Legislature cannot be convened), against domestic Violence.

ARTICLE 5

The Congress, whenever two thirds of both Houses shall deem it necessary, shall propose Amendments to this Constitution, or, on the Application of the Legislatures of two thirds of the several States, shall call a Convention for proposing Amendments, which, in either Case, shall be valid to all Intents and Purposes, as Part of this Constitution, when ratified by the Legislatures of three fourths of the several States, or by Conventions in three fourths thereof, as the one or the other Mode of Ratification may be proposed by the Congress; Provided that no Amendment which may be made prior to the Year One thousand eight hundred and eight shall in any Manner affect the first and fourth Clauses in the Ninth Section of the first Article; and that no State, without its Consent, shall be deprived of its equal Suffrage in the Senate.

ARTICLE 6

All Debts contracted and Engagements entered into, before the Adoption of this Constitution, shall be as valid against the United States under this Constitution, as under the Confederation.

This Constitution, and the Laws of the United States which shall be made in Pursuance thereof; and all Treaties made, or which shall be made, under the Authority of the United States, shall be the supreme Law of the Land; and the Judges in every State shall be bound thereby, any Thing in the Constitution or Laws of any State to the Contrary notwithstanding.

The Senators and Representatives before mentioned, and the Members of the several State Legislatures, and all executive and judicial Officers, both of the United States and of the several States, shall be bound by Oath or Affirmation, to support this Constitution; but no religious Test shall ever be required as a Qualification to any Office or public Trust under the United States.

ARTICLE 7

The Ratification of the Conventions of nine States, shall be sufficient for the Establishment of this Constitution between the States so ratifying the Same.

The Word, "the," being interlined between the seventh and eighth Lines of the first Page, the Word "Thirty" being partly written on an Erasure in the fifteenth Line of the first Page, The Words "is tried" being interlined between the thirty second and thirty third Lines of the first

Page and the Word "the" being interlined between the forty third and forty fourth Lines of the second Page.

Attest William Jackson Secretary

Done in Convention by the Unanimous Consent of the States present the Seventeenth Day of September in the Year of our Lord one thousand seven hundred and Eighty seven and of the Independence of the United States of America the Twelfth In witness whereof We have hereunto subscribed our Names,

G. Washington
    Presidt and deputy from
    Virginia

Delaware
    Geo: Read
    Gunning Bedford jun
    John Dickinson
    Richard Bassett
    Jaco: Broom

Maryland
    James McHenry
    Dan of St Thos. Jenifer
    Danl. Carroll

Virginia
    John Blair
    James Madison Jr.

North Carolina
    Wm. Blount
    Richd. Dobbs Spaight
    Hu Williamson

South Carolina
    J. Rutledge
    Charles Cotesworth Pinckney
    Charles Pinckney
    Pierce Butler

Georgia
    William Few
    Abr Baldwin

New Hampshire
    John Langdon
    Nicholas Gilman

Massachusetts
    Nathaniel Gorham
    Rufus King

Connecticut
    Wm. Saml. Johnson
    Roger Sherman

New York
    Alexander Hamilton

New Jersey	Pennsylvania
Wil: Livingston	B Franklin
David Brearley	Thomas Mifflin
Wm. Paterson	Robt. Morris
Jona: Dayton	Geo. Clymer
	Thos. FitzSimons
	Jared Ingersoll
	James Wilson
	Gouv Morris

ARTICLES OF AMENDMENT

Amendment 1

Congress shall make no law respecting an establishment of religion, or prohibiting the free exercise thereof; or abridging the freedom of speech, or of the press; or the right of the people peaceably to assemble, and to petition the Government for a redress of grievances.

Amendment 2

A well regulated Militia, being necessary to the security of a free State, the right of the people to keep and bear Arms, shall not be infringed.

Amendment 3

No Soldier shall, in time of peace be quartered in any house, without the consent of the Owner, nor in time of war, but in a manner to be prescribed by law.

Amendment 4

The right of the people to be secure in their persons, houses, papers, and effects, against unreasonable searches and seizures, shall not be violated, and no Warrants shall issue, but upon probable cause, supported by Oath or affirmation, and particularly describing the place to be searched, and the persons or things to be seized.

Amendment 5

No person shall be held to answer for a capital, or otherwise infamous crime, unless on a presentment or indictment of a Grand Jury, except in cases arising in the land or naval forces, or in the Militia, when in actual service in time of War or public danger; nor shall any person be subject for the same offense to be twice put in jeopardy of life or limb; nor shall be compelled in any criminal case to be a witness against himself, nor be deprived of life, liberty, or property, without due process of law; nor shall private property be taken for public use, without just compensation.

Amendment 6

In all criminal prosecutions, the accused shall enjoy the right to a speedy and public trial, by an impartial jury of the State and district wherein the crime shall have been committed, which district shall have been previously ascertained by law, and to be informed of the nature and cause of the accusation; to be confronted with the witnesses against him; to have compulsory process for obtaining witnesses in his favor, and to have the Assistance of Counsel for his defense.

Amendment 7

In Suits at common law, where the value in controversy shall exceed twenty dollars, the right of trial by jury shall be preserved, and no fact tried by a jury, shall be otherwise re-examined in any Court of the United States, than according to the rules of the common law.

Amendment 8

Excessive bail shall not be required, nor excessive fines imposed, nor cruel and unusual punishments inflicted.

Amendment 9

The enumeration in the Constitution, of certain rights, shall not be construed to deny or disparage others retained by the people.

Amendment 10

The powers not delegated to the United States by the Constitution, nor prohibited by it to the States, are reserved to the States respectively, or to the people.

Amendment 11

The Judicial power of the United States shall not be construed to extend to any suit in law or equity, commenced or prosecuted against one of the United States by Citizens of another State, or by Citizens or Subjects of any Foreign State.

Amendment 12

The Electors shall meet in their respective states and vote by ballot for President and Vice-President, one of whom, at least, shall not be an inhabitant of the same state with themselves; they shall name in their ballots the person voted for as President, and in distinct ballots the person voted for as Vice-President, and they shall make distinct lists of all persons voted for as President, and of all persons voted for as Vice-President, and of the number of votes for each, which lists they shall sign and certify, and transmit sealed to the seat of the government of the United States, directed to the President of the Senate;—the President of the Senate shall, in the presence of the Senate and House of Representatives, open all the certificates and the votes shall then be counted;—The person having the greatest number of votes for President, shall be the President, if such number be a majority of the whole number of Electors appointed; and if no person have such majority, then from the persons having the highest numbers not exceeding three on the list of those voted for as President, the House of Representatives shall choose immediately, by ballot, the President. But in choosing the President, the votes shall be taken by states, the representation from each state having one vote; a quorum for this purpose shall consist of a member or members from two-thirds of the states, and a majority of all the states shall be necessary to a choice. And if the House of Representatives shall not choose a President whenever the right of choice shall devolve upon them, before the fourth day of March next following, then the Vice-President shall act as President, as in case of the death or other constitutional disability of the President.—[10] The person having the greatest number of votes as Vice-President, shall be the Vice-President, if such number be a majority of the whole number of Electors appointed, and if no person have a majority, then from the two highest numbers on the list, the Senate shall choose the Vice-President; a quorum for the purpose shall consist of two-thirds of the whole number of Senators, and a majority of the whole number shall be necessary to a choice. But no person constitutionally ineligible to the office of President shall be eligible to that of Vice-President of the United States.

Amendment 13

Section 1. Neither slavery nor involuntary servitude, except as a punishment for crime whereof the party shall have been duly convicted, shall exist within the United States, or any place subject to their jurisdiction.

Section 2. Congress shall have power to enforce this article by appropriate legislation.

Amendment 14

Section 1. All persons born or naturalized in the United States, and subject to the jurisdiction thereof, are citizens of the United States and of the State wherein they reside. No State shall make or enforce any law which shall abridge the privileges or immunities of citizens of the United States; nor shall any State deprive any person of life, liberty, or property, without due process of law; nor deny to any person within its jurisdiction the equal protection of the laws.

Section 2. Representatives shall be apportioned among the several States according to their respective numbers, counting the whole number of persons in each State, excluding Indians not taxed. But when the right to vote at any election for the choice of electors for President and Vice-President of the United States, Representatives in Congress, the Executive and Judicial officers of a State, or the members of the Legislature thereof, is denied to any of the male inhabitants of such State, being twenty-one years of age,[11] and citizens of the United States, or in any way abridged, except for participation in rebellion, or other crime, the basis of representation therein shall be reduced in the proportion which the number of such male citizens shall bear to the whole number of male citizens twenty-one years of age in such State.

Section 3. No person shall be a Senator or Representative in Congress, or elector of President and Vice-President, or hold any office, civil or military, under the United States, or under any State, who, having previously taken an oath, as a member of Congress, or as an officer of the United States, or as a member of any State legislature, or as an executive or judicial officer of any State, to support the Constitution of the United States, shall have engaged in insurrection or rebellion against the same, or given aid or comfort to the enemies thereof. But Congress may by a vote of two-thirds of each House, remove such disability.

Section 4. The validity of the public debt of the United States, authorized by law, including debts incurred for payment of pensions and bounties for services in suppressing insurrection or rebellion, shall not be questioned. But neither the United States nor any State shall assume or pay any debt or obligation incurred in aid of insurrection or rebellion against the United States, or any claim for the loss or emancipation of any slave; but all such debts, obligations and claims shall be held illegal and void.

Section 5. The Congress shall have the power to enforce, by appropriate legislation, the provisions of this article.

Amendment 15

Section 1. The right of citizens of the United States to vote shall not be denied or abridged by the United States or by any State on account of race, color, or previous condition of servitude—

Section 2. The Congress shall have the power to enforce this article by appropriate legislation.

Amendment 16

The Congress shall have power to lay and collect taxes on incomes, from whatever source derived, without apportionment among the several States, and without regard to any census or enumeration.

Amendment 17

The Senate of the United States shall be composed of two Senators from each State, elected by the people thereof, for six years; and each Senator shall have one vote. The electors in each State shall have the qualifications requisite for electors of the most numerous branch of the State legislatures.

When vacancies happen in the representation of any State in the Senate, the executive authority of such State shall issue writs of election to fill such vacancies: Provided, That the legislature of any State may empower the executive thereof to make temporary appointments until the people fill the vacancies by election as the legislature may direct.

This amendment shall not be so construed as to affect the election or term of any Senator chosen before it becomes valid as part of the Constitution.

Amendment 18

Section 1. After one year from the ratification of this article the manufacture, sale, or transportation of intoxicating liquors within, the importation thereof into, or the exportation thereof from the United States and all territory subject to the jurisdiction thereof for beverage purposes is hereby prohibited.

Section 2. The Congress and the several States shall have concurrent power to enforce this article by appropriate legislation.

Section 3. This article shall be inoperative unless it shall have been ratified as an amendment to the Constitution by the legislatures of the several States, as provided in the Constitution, within seven years from the date of the submission hereof to the States by the Congress.[12]

Amendment 19

The right of citizens of the United States to vote shall not be denied or abridged by the United States or by any State on account of sex.

Congress shall have power to enforce this article by appropriate legislation.

Amendment 20

Section 1. The terms of the President and the Vice President shall end at noon on the 20th day of January, and the terms of Senators and Representatives at noon on the 3d day of January, of the years in which such terms would have ended if this article had not been ratified; and the terms of their successors shall then begin.

Section 2. The Congress shall assemble at least once in every year, and such meeting shall begin at noon on the 3d day of January, unless they shall by law appoint a different day.

Section 3. If, at the time fixed for the beginning of the term of the President, the President elect shall have died, the Vice President elect shall become President. If a President shall not have been chosen before the time fixed for the beginning of his term, or if the President elect shall have failed to qualify, then the Vice President elect shall act as President until a President shall have qualified; and the Congress may by law provide for the case wherein neither a President elect nor a Vice President shall have qualified, declaring who shall then act as President, or the manner in which one who is to act shall be selected, and such person shall act accordingly until a President or Vice President shall have qualified.

Section 4. The Congress may by law provide for the case of the death of any of the persons from whom the House of Representatives may choose a President whenever the right of choice shall have devolved upon them, and for the case of the death of any of the persons from whom the Senate may choose a Vice President whenever the right of choice shall have devolved upon them.

Section 5. Sections 1 and 2 shall take effect on the 15th day of October following the ratification of this article.

Section 6. This article shall be inoperative unless it shall have been ratified as an amendment to the Constitution by the legislatures of three-fourths of the several States within seven years from the date of its submission.

Amendment 21

Section 1. The eighteenth article of amendment to the Constitution of the United States is hereby repealed.

Section 2. The transportation or importation into any State, Territory, or Possession of the United States for delivery or use therein of intoxicating liquors, in violation of the laws thereof, is hereby prohibited.

Section 3. This article shall be inoperative unless it shall have been ratified as an amendment to the Constitution by conventions in the several States, as provided in the Constitution, within seven years from the date of the submission hereof to the States by the Congress.

Amendment 22

Section 1. No person shall be elected to the office of the President more than twice, and no person who has held the office of President, or acted as President, for more than two years of a term to which some other person was elected President shall be elected to the office of President more than once. But this Article shall not apply to any person holding the office of President when this Article was proposed by Congress, and shall not prevent any person who may be holding the office of President, or acting as President, during the term within which this Article becomes operative from holding the office of President or acting as President during the remainder of such term.

Section 2. This article shall be inoperative unless it shall have been ratified as an amendment to the Constitution by the legislatures of three-fourths of the several States within seven years from the date of its submission to the States by the Congress.

Amendment 23

Section 1. The District constituting the seat of Government of the United States shall appoint in such manner as Congress may direct:

A number of electors of President and Vice President equal to the whole number of Senators and Representatives in Congress to which the District would be entitled if it were a State, but in no event more than the least populous State; they shall be in addition to those appointed by the States, but they shall be considered, for the purposes of the election of President and Vice President, to be electors appointed by a State; and they shall meet in the District and perform such duties as provided by the twelfth article of amendment.

Section 2. The Congress shall have power to enforce this article by appropriate legislation.

Amendment 24

Section 1. The right of citizens of the United States to vote in any primary or other election for President or Vice President, for electors for President or Vice President, or for Senator or Representative in Congress, shall not be denied or abridged by the United States or any State by reason of failure to pay poll tax or other tax.

Section 2. The Congress shall have power to enforce this article by appropriate legislation.

Amendment 25

Section 1. In case of the removal of the President from office or of his death or resignation, the Vice President shall become President.

Section 2. Whenever there is a vacancy in the office of the Vice President, the President shall nominate a Vice President who shall take office upon confirmation by a majority vote of both Houses of Congress.

Section 3. Whenever the President transmits to the President pro tempore of the Senate and the Speaker of the House of Representatives his written declaration that he is unable to discharge the powers and duties of his office, and until he transmits to them a written declaration to the contrary, such powers and duties shall be discharged by the Vice President as Acting President.

Section 4. Whenever the Vice President and a majority of either the principal officers of the executive departments or of such other body as Congress may by law provide, transmit to the President pro tempore of the Senate and the Speaker of the House of Representatives their written declaration that the President is unable to discharge the powers and duties of his office, the Vice President shall immediately assume the powers and duties of the office as Acting President.

Thereafter, when the President transmits to the President pro tempore of the Senate and the Speaker of the House of Representatives his written declaration that no inability exists, he shall resume the powers and duties of his office unless the Vice President and a majority of either the principal officers of the executive department or of such other body as Congress may by law provide, transmit within four days to the President pro tempore of the Senate and the Speaker of the House of Representatives their written declaration that the President is unable to discharge the powers and duties of his office. Thereupon Congress shall decide the issue, assembling within forty-eight hours for that purpose if not in session. If the Congress, within twenty-one days after receipt of the latter written declaration, or, if Congress is not in session, within twenty-one days after Congress is required to assemble, determines by two-thirds vote of both Houses that the President is unable to discharge the powers and duties of his office, the Vice President shall continue to discharge the same as Acting President; otherwise, the President shall resume the powers and duties of his office.

Amendment 26

Section 1. The right of citizens of the United States, who are eighteen years of age or older, to vote shall not be denied or abridged by the United States or by any State on account of age.

Section 2. The Congress shall have power to enforce this article by appropriate legislation.

Amendment 27

No law, varying the compensation for the services of the Senators and Representatives, shall take effect, until an election of representatives shall have intervened.

NOTES

1. Modified by the Fourteenth Amendment.
2. Modified by the Seventeenth Amendment.
3. Also modified by the Seventeenth Amendment.
4. Modified by the Twentieth Amendment; part of the Twelfth Amendment was also superseded by the Twentieth.
5. Modified by the Sixteenth Amendment.
6. Partially superseded by the Twelfth Amendment.
7. Affected by the Twenty-fifth Amendment.
8. Modified by the Eleventh Amendment.
9. Superseded by the Thirteenth Amendment.
10. Superseded by the Twentieth Amendment.
11. Modified by the Twenty-sixth Amendment.
12. The Eighteenth Amendment was repealed by the Twenty-first.

IN CONGRESS, JULY 4, 1776
THE UNANIMOUS DECLARATION OF THE
THIRTEEN UNITED STATES OF AMERICA

When in the Course of human events it becomes necessary for one people to dissolve the political bands which have connected them with another and to assume among the powers of the earth, the separate and equal station to which the Laws of Nature and of Nature's God entitle them, a decent respect to the opinions of mankind requires that they should declare the causes which impel them to the separation.

We hold these truths to be self-evident, that all men are created equal, that they are endowed by their Creator with certain unalienable Rights, that among these are Life, Liberty and the pursuit of Happiness.—That to secure these rights, Governments are instituted among Men, deriving their just powers from the consent of the governed,—That whenever any Form of Government becomes destructive of these ends, it is the Right of the People to alter or to abolish it, and to institute new Government, laying its foundation on such principles and organizing its powers in such form, as to them shall seem most likely to effect their Safety and Happiness. Prudence, indeed, will dictate that Governments long established should not be changed for light and transient causes; and accordingly all experience hath shewn that mankind are more disposed to suffer, while evils are sufferable than to right themselves by abolishing the forms to which they are accustomed. But when a long train of abuses and usurpations, pursuing invariably the same Object evinces a design to reduce them under absolute Despotism, it is their right, it is their duty, to throw off such Government, and to provide new Guards for their future security.—Such has been the patient sufferance of these Colonies; and such is now the necessity which constrains them to alter their former Systems of Government. The history of the present King of Great Britain is a history of repeated injuries and usurpations, all having in direct object the establishment of an absolute Tyranny over these States. To prove this, let Facts be submitted to a candid world.

He has refuted his Assent to Laws, the most wholesome and necessary for the public good.

He has forbidden his Governors to pass Laws of immediate and pressing importance, unless suspended in their operation till his Assent should be obtained; and when so suspended, he has utterly neglected to attend to them.

He has refused to pass other Laws for the accommodation of large districts of people, unless those people would relinquish the right of Representation in the Legislature, a right inestimable to them and formidable to tyrants only.

He has called together legislative bodies at places unusual, uncomfortable, and distant from the depository of their Public Records, for the sole purpose of fatiguing them into compliance with his measures.

He has dissolved Representative Houses repeatedly, for opposing with manly firmness his invasions on the rights of the people.

He has refused for a long time, after such dissolutions, to cause others to be elected, whereby the Legislative Powers, incapable of Annihilation, have returned to the People at large for their exercise; the State remaining in the mean time exposed to all the dangers of invasion from without, and convulsions within.

He has endeavoured to prevent the population of these States; for that purpose obstructing the Laws for Naturalization of Foreigners; refusing to pass others to encourage their migrations hither, and raising the conditions of new Appropriations of Lands.

He has obstructed the Administration of Justice by refusing his Assent to Laws for establishing Judiciary Powers.

He has made Judges dependent on his Will alone for the tenure of their offices, and the amount and payment of their salaries.

He has erected a multitude of New Offices, and sent hither swarms of Officers to harass our people and eat out their substance.

He has kept among us, in times of peace, Standing Armies without the Consent of our legislatures.

He has affected to render the Military independent of and superior to the Civil Power.

He has combined with others to subject us to a jurisdiction foreign to our constitution, and unacknowledged by our laws; giving his Assent to their Acts of pretended Legislation:

For quartering large bodies of armed troops among us:

For protecting them, by a mock Trial from punishment for any Murders which they should commit on the Inhabitants of these States:

For cutting off our Trade with all parts of the world:

For imposing Taxes on us without our Consent:

For depriving us in many cases, of the benefit of Trial by Jury:

For transporting us beyond Seas to be tried for pretended offences:

For abolishing the free System of English Laws in a neighbouring Province, establishing therein an Arbitrary government, and enlarging its Boundaries so as to render it at once an example and fit instrument for introducing the same absolute rule into these Colonies

For taking away our Charters, abolishing our most valuable Laws and altering fundamentally the Forms of our Governments:

For suspending our own Legislatures, and declaring themselves invested with power to legislate for us in all cases whatsoever.

He has abdicated Government here, by declaring us out of his Protection and waging War against us.

He has plundered our seas, ravaged our coasts, burnt our towns, and destroyed the lives of our people.

He is at this time transporting large Armies of foreign Mercenaries to compleat the works of death, desolation, and tyranny, already begun with circumstances of Cruelty & Perfidy scarcely paralleled in the most barbarous ages, and totally unworthy the Head of a civilized nation.

He has constrained our fellow Citizens taken Captive on the high Seas to bear Arms against their Country, to become the executioners of their friends and Brethren, or to fall themselves by their Hands.

He has excited domestic insurrections amongst us, and has endeavoured to bring on the inhabitants of our frontiers, the merciless Indian Savages whose known rule of warfare, is an undistinguished destruction of all ages, sexes and conditions.

In every stage of these Oppressions We have Petitioned for Redress in the most humble terms: Our repeated Petitions have been answered only by repeated injury. A Prince, whose character is thus marked by every act which may define a Tyrant, is unfit to be the ruler of a free people.

Nor have We been wanting in attentions to our British brethren. We have warned them from time to time of attempts by their legislature to extend an unwarrantable jurisdiction over us. We have reminded them of the circumstances of our emigration and settlement here. We have appealed to their native justice and magnanimity, and we have conjured them by the ties of our common kindred. to disavow these usurpations, which would inevitably interrupt our connections and correspondence. They too have been deaf to the voice of justice and of consanguinity. We must, therefore, acquiesce in the necessity, which denounces our Separation, and hold them, as we hold the rest of mankind, Enemies in War, in Peace Friends.

We, therefore, the Representatives of the United States of America, in General Congress, Assembled, appealing to the Supreme Judge of the world for the rectitude of our intentions, do, in the Name, and by Authority of the good People of these Colonies, solemnly publish and declare, That these United Colonies are, and of Right ought to be Free and Independent States, that they are Absolved from all Allegiance to the British Crown, and that all political connection between them and the State of Great Britain, is and ought to be totally dissolved; and that as Free and Independent States, they have full Power to levy War, conclude Peace contract Alliances, establish Commerce, and to do all other Acts and Things which Independent States may of right do.—And for the support of this Declaration, with a firm reliance on the protection of Divine Providence, we mutually pledge to each other our Lives, our Fortunes and our sacred Honor.

—John Hancock

New Hampshire:
Josiah Bartlett, William Whipple, Matthew Thornton

Massachusetts:
John Hancock, Samuel Adams, John Adams,
Robert Treat Paine, Elbridge Gerry

Rhode Island:
Stephen Hopkins, William Ellery

Connecticut:
Roger Sherman, Samuel Huntington,
William Williams, Oliver Wolcott

New York:
William Floyd, Philip Livingston, Francis Lewis, Lewis Morris

New Jersey:
Richard Stockton, John Witherspoon, Francis Hopkinson,
John Hart, Abraham Clark

Pennsylvania:
Robert Morris, Benjamin Rush, Benjamin Franklin,
John Morton, George Clymer, James Smith,
George Taylor, James Wilson, George Ross

Delaware:
Caesar Rodney, George Read, Thomas McKean

Maryland:
Samuel Chase, William Paca, Thomas Stone,
Charles Carroll of Carrollton

Virginia:
George Wythe, Richard Henry Lee, Thomas Jefferson,
Benjamin Harrison, Thomas Nelson, Jr.,
Francis Lightfoot Lee, Carter Braxton

North Carolina:
William Hooper, Joseph Hewes, John Penn

South Carolina:
Edward Rutledge, Thomas Heyward, Jr.,
Thomas Lynch, Jr., Arthur Middleton

Georgia:
Button Gwinnett, Lyman Hall, George Walton

ABOUT THE AUTHOR

JUDGE ANDREW P. NAPOLITANO

 Andrew P. Napolitano graduated from Princeton University in 1972 and the University of Notre Dame Law School in 1975. He is the youngest life-tenured Superior Court judge in the history of the State of New Jersey. For eleven years, Judge Napolitano was adjunct professor of law at Seton Hall Law School, where he taught constitutional law and jurisprudence and was voted most outstanding professor in three different academic years. He has been the Senior Judicial Analyst for the Fox News Channel since 1998. He broadcasts nationwide on Fox every weekday on *The Big Story*; he co-hosts *Fox & Friends*; he is a regular on *The O'Reilly Factor*; and he co-hosts *Brian and the Judge*, heard daily nationwide on Fox Radio. Judge Napolitano also lectures nationally and has been published in the *New York Times*, the *Wall Street Journal*, the *Los Angeles Times*, the *St. Louis Post-Dispatch*, the *New York Sun*, the *Baltimore Sun*, the (New London) *Day*, the *Seton Hall Law Review*, the *New Jersey Law Journal*, and the *Newark Star-Ledger*.

Judge Andrew P. Napolitano lays bare the twisted legal history of racism in America.

"All men are created equal and endowed by their Creator with certain inalienable rights" wedded the American soul to the concept that freedom comes from our humanity, not from the government. But American governments legally suspended the free will of blacks for 150 years, and then denied blacks equal protection of the law for another 150 years. How did this happen in America, how were the Constitution and laws of the land twisted so as to institutionalize racism, and how did it or will it end? In a refreshingly candid book, *Dred Scott's Revenge: A Legal History of Race and Freedom In America*, Judge Andrew P. Napolitano takes a no-holds-barred look at the role of the government in the denial of freedoms based on race.

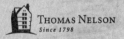

What new crisis will the federal government manufacture in order to acquire more power over individuals? What new **LIES** will it tell?

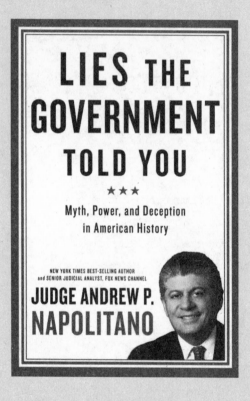

Throughout our history, the federal government has lied to send our children off to war, lied to take our money, lied to steal our property, lied to gain our trust, and lied to enhance its power over us. Not only does the government lie to us, we lie to ourselves. We won't admit that each time we let the government get away with misleading us, we are allowing it to increase in size and power and decrease our personal liberty. This book attacks the culture in government that facilitates lying, and it challenges readers to recognize that culture, to confront it, and to be rid of it.

Available March 2010

Lies the Government Told You

INTRODUCTION

During the 1980 presidential campaign, a joke made the rounds in the Reagan camp: George Washington, Richard Nixon, and Jimmy Carter die and go to Heaven. In a chance meeting about how they got there, Washington boasts "I never told a lie." Not to be outdone, Nixon proclaims "I never told the truth." A determined Carter can't resist: "I never knew the difference!"

What is a lie? What is the truth? What is the difference?

One could not begin to count all the words, ink, and paper spent addressing those three questions, even though the answers are implicated in almost every thought and every word and every act that everyone perceives, utters, and engages upon every day of our adult lives.

Truth is identity between intellect and reality; and a lie is a knowing and intentional violation of the truth. The difference between the two depends on whether one is in the governing class or the governed class.

We have all come to expect some lying in our lives, and have engaged in lying to some extent; perhaps to avoid or postpone a crisis, or to serve a higher good, or because telling a lie was easier

245

under the circumstances than telling the truth, and the consequences of the lie were harmless. This is all normal human behavior, and it can range from being necessary for survival to being innocuous.

If a ship captain is secretly ferrying innocents from slavery to freedom, and his ship is stopped on the high seas by agents of the government that enslaved his passengers, should he lie about their true identities? When a co-worker asks how you are during a miserable day, should you lie to avoid a painful and useless conversation? Can silence be a lie when one has a lawful or moral duty to tell the truth? These are issues with which we wrestle almost every day.

In a free society, we expect the government to wrestle with them as well. The government in America does not. It is not concerned with truth. It lies to us regularly, consistently, systematically, and daily on matters great and small, and it prosecutes and jails those who lie to it. For example, a male drug dealer with a heavy foreign accent and minimal understanding of English stupidly tells an FBI agent that his name is Nancy Reagan, and he is arrested, prosecuted, and jailed for lying to the government. Another FBI agent tells the cultural guru Martha Stewart, in an informal conversation in the presence of others, that she is not the target of a federal criminal probe, and she replies that she did not sell a certain stock on a certain day. They both lied; but she went to jail, and the FBI agent kept his job.

What is it about the government and its agents and employees that they can lie to us with impunity, but we are exposed to the risk of going to jail if we lie to them?

Throughout this book, I will suggest answers to these and similar questions. As I do so, you'll see a chip on my shoulder. I am angry that we allow the government to lie to us, that we expect it to do so, and even take comfort in the illusions created thereby. When I told friends about the title of this book, I frequently joked that it would be 4,000 pages in length. Most laughed; but none doubted that there have been enough government lies to consume that many printed pages.

When you recall that the Declaration of Independence and the Constitution of the United States mandate a free and open society, one in which *the government works for us,* you can see where the chip on my shoulder came from. It is morally reprehensible for any government to lie to anyone over whom it has lawful authority. But in a free and open society where *we are the employers, and the government workers are the employees,* every government employee—from a public school janitor to a state governor, from a soldier to an FBI agent, from a cop to the President—has a lawful obligation to be truthful to his or her employers. It is utterly and completely and unconditionally unacceptable to treat as normal that they should lie to us.

And yet, treat it as normal we do. Just look at the names of the chapters in this book—from "All Men Are Created Equal" to "Congress Shall Make No Law . . . Abridging the Freedom of Speech." from "All Men Are Innocent Until Proven Guilty" to "Your Boys Are Not Going to Be Sent into Any Foreign Wars" to "We Don't Torture"—and you will see the stuff of which historical myth is made. Every one of those well-known, well-worn, well-stated canards are goals the government has never reached but claims it has. Each has become a bald-faced lie, a perpetrated myth, a grasp at power, a monstrous deception: And most of us recognize that.

Why do we believe government-generated myths? Why do we allow the use of myth to enhance government power? Why do we condone the government's use of deception to crush our freedom, steal our property, and destroy our lives? And how does the government get away with all this?

These are the questions we will explore in the coming pages, as we tear through American history from 1776 to 2010, and expose the use of myth to seize power and the power of deception to delude the public. When the public is deluded by the very folks it has hired to defend our freedom, the delusion interferes with that freedom by denying us accurate information with which we can decide in whose hands we should repose government power. Would Americans have re-elected FDR had they known that he *caused* the attack on Pearl Harbor? Would voters have chosen LBJ, the supposed "peace candidate" in 1964, had they known he was *secretly planning* to ramp up the Vietnam war? Would George W. Bush have been re-elected in 2004 if we knew he was illegally spying on us, concocting evidence for war, torturing innocents, and *lying* about it?

Government lies take on a life of their own since they breed more lies to substantiate the original lies. Government lies induce government law-breaking, and government law-breaking means someone is suffering a loss of life, liberty, or property because of some event not caused by the person suffering; and it also means that the law breaker walks free in the corridors of power to strike again.

Government lies are a direct assault on freedom because, if believed, if accepted as truth, the lies dupe individuals into making choices they would not make were the truth known. Government lies seduce us into surrendering freedom and accepting unlawful behavior and irretrievable loss as somehow warranted, and they establish a precedent for similar thefts of freedom and personal loss in the future.

In my previous books, I have targeted government excess. In *Constitutional Chaos: What Happens When the Government Breaks Its Own Laws,* I argued that government lawbreaking is a serious, yet hidden problem recognized primarily by those who benefit from or are victimized by it, and if unchecked, will lead to tyranny.

In *The Constitution in Exile: How the Federal Government Has Seized Power by Rewriting the Supreme Law of the Land*, I made the case that the feds have systematically stolen power from the States and freedom from individuals, under the guise of interpreting the Constitution, and much of that power and many of those freedoms will be impossible to re-claim. In *A Nation of Sheep*, I showed that government in America hates freedom, that it defends its power and not our rights, even though our rights are natural, come from our humanity, and as Jefferson stated, are "inalienable." In *Dred Scott's Revenge: A Legal History of Race and Freedom in America*, I demonstrated that any government that thinks it can suspend the free will of the innocent is fatal to life, fatal to freedom, and breeds horrors that can last for centuries.

In the pages that follow, I continue with my theme that the-government–is–not–your–friend. The lies told to us by our own government, and accepted by our grandparents and our parents and our children, have destroyed the lives, stolen the freedom, crushed the God–given rights, and seized the property of those who got in the way of official government deception. Why have our governments rejected America's first principles of individual freedom, guaranteed rights, limited government, free enterprise, private property, and the right to be left alone? And why have they denied doing so?

Come with me now on a tour of myth, power, and deception in America; woven into the fabric of our history, perpetrated even as you read this, and accepted by millions as the norm.